EP Sport Series

* All About Judo
* Badminton
* Basketball
  Conditioning for Sport
  Cricket
  Field Athletics
* Football
* Golf
  Hockey for Men and Women
  Improve your Riding
  Learning to Swim
  Modern Riding
* Netball
* Orienteering
  Rock Climbing
  Sailing
  Snooker
* Squash Rackets
  Start Motor Cruising
* Table Tennis
* Tennis up to Tournament
    Standard
* Track Athletics
  Underwater Swimming
  Volleyball
  Wildwater Canoeing
  Women's Gymnastics

At the time of publication of
this edition the asterisked
titles are available in
paperback as well as hardback

ep sport

improve your riding

dressage
jumping
cross~country

Albert Brandl

translated by

Lt. Col. R.L.V. ffrench-Blake

Introduction

After early basic instruction, the rider, still lacking experience, is often left to his own devices. More and more riders are becoming interested in competitive riding, and specialising in dressage, show-jumping or eventing. To succeed in competition means that the sport which started as a hobby must now be approached at professional standards, which means training. Training involves systematic preparation to achieve the best possible performance of horse and rider, and must be based on extensive theoretical and practical knowledge. It will only be possible to spend a limited time under the eye of the instructor, so that riders are obliged to depend largely on their own resources.

This book sets out, therefore, to advise the rider both about the schooling of his horse, and about the requirements of special training.

No book can deal with all matters of equitation—this one is no exception; it contains little new material, and does not set out to replace other proven works.

What *is* new is the format of this manual. Using sound instructional principles the author assembles photographs, drawings and picture sequences, many of world-class riders at the Munich Olympics, to illustrate the most important points of technique.

ISBN 0 7158 0634 3 (cased edition)
ISBN 0 7158 0645 9 (limp edition)

German edition first published by Verlagsgesellschaft mbH, Munich, 1974

English edition published by EP Publishing Ltd, East Ardsley, Wakefield, West Yorkshire, 1978

Text set in 11/12 pt Monophoto Univers, printed by photolithography, and bound in Great Britain by G. Beard & Son Ltd, Brighton, Sussex

Acknowledgements

The publishers would like to thank the Midland Bank Public Relations Department for their help in supplying the cover transparency. The cover picture shows Miss Annabel Scrimgeour on Snow Justice and is reproduced by courtesy of the photographer, John Elliot. All photographs and diagrams inside the book are reproduced from the original German material.

About the Author

Albert Brandl's father, a riding instructor, gave him his first horse at the age of ten, and it was not long before Albert was competing in major events.

In 1956 he was employed as a trainer and instructor at Warendorf, later moving as manager to the Rhineland Riding and Driving School, where his talent for improving both horses and pupils raised the school to the highest standards. He rode successfully as a competitor in Three-day Events, Show-jumping and Advanced Dressage, and was awarded the Gold Medal for Riding. Everything that Albert Brandl describes in this book is therefore based on the practical experience of an active rider, who has handed on his knowledge successfully to his pupils.

Preface

by Lt. Col. R. L. V. ffrench-Blake

My part in the production of this book has been merely that of translator. Assisted by Nigel Suffield-Jones of Bradfield College, who did the 'donkeywork' by making a literal translation, I have attempted to interpret Herr Brandl's text into a language comprehensible to students of riding in this country.

There are certain inevitable difficulties in translations of any sort. If the translator attempts to produce an elegant style, he may be forced too far away from the original thoughts of the author; if, on the other hand, the translator is too literal, the text may read like a comedy sketch caricaturing the foreigner. Then there is the matter of word meanings—'When I use a word', said Humpty-Dumpty, 'it means just what I choose it to mean—neither more nor less.' There are certain words used in German riding instruction which are exceptionally difficult to translate into English, since, like Humpty-Dumpty's 'portmanteau' words, they contain more than one meaning packed into the same word.

Takt for instance means both 'time' in the sense of 'beating time', and 'rhythm'—not quite the same thing.

Losgelassenheit has an element of freedom as well as relaxation.

Schwung means energy, swing, spring, and impulsion. The most difficult of all, and one most frequently heard, is *Durchlässigkeit*—literally 'letting-throughness' (it can even be used of a leaky macintosh)—but in riding terms it describes the way in which impulsion, generated in the hindquarters, is transmitted *through* a supple, swinging back, *through* the flexed neck, into the mouth, where it is accepted softly by the rider's hand. All this in one word! The best one can do is 'willing obedience', 'supple obedience', 'soft acceptance' and so on, depending on the context in which the word is used. In addition, translation is made more difficult by a feeling that the *'Durchlässigkeit'* of a horse varies in different ways, according to the level of training.

Another interesting point of difference in British and German is the word for the rider's leg as used in giving the aids. The Germans use the word *Schenkel* (which means 'thigh') for all leg aids; the *Unterschenkel* or lower leg is seldom mentioned except when it is in the wrong place. One wonders if there is a basic difference of thought between the two countries regarding the rider's seat and application of the aids?

I had hoped to visit Herr Brandl in Germany and to have discussed some of these points with him, but unfortunately, just before my visit he had a bad accident, and was in hospital. It is sad to say that he never recovered from this accident and died in October, 1977.

There is much good advice in this book. I hope that I have succeeded in transmitting Herr Brandl's intentions to the reader; I stress again that the text is a straightforward translation—any freer interpretations are shown under the words 'translator's note'.

5

The Three-day Event

Physical Training for the Rider

General Principles of Training

The daily ride is the unit from which the training programme of both horse and rider is constructed. On it is built a regular system which should be followed methodically for days, weeks, months and years. This system comprises **basic schooling, build-up training** and **continuation training.**
Basic schooling is of paramount importance; every single training period must follow its principles towards the ultimate goal. That is, complete control of the horse by the rider in the dressage arena, cross-country course or jumping ring.
Schooling must be devised so that the horse's natural movements are preserved and improved under the rider; faults in schooling will create faults in gait, responsiveness and obedience in the horse. Six main points of the system of schooling must run in an unbroken thread through every training period:

- Rhythm
- Relaxation and suppleness
- Acceptance of the bit
- Impulsion
- Straightness
- Collection

Rhythm

Rhythm involves regularity of the basic paces: walk, trot and canter.
The walk is a calm pace in four-time, with eight stages of locomotion (see diagram). Rhythm can be lost if the horse becomes tense from too strong rein-action by the rider or if urged beyond its natural ability to step out. The result can be an amble or 'camel-walk', both legs on the same side being carried forward together.
The trot is a two-time pace with four stages of locomotion. Here also a horse can lose rhythm if too much is demanded; the steps become uneven, or the horse hurries and tends to 'run'.
The canter is a three-time pace in six stages. If the rider attempts to strike off too strongly in the canter, with too much influence of the hands, the hindquarters of the horse will be prevented from moving forward freely, and the canter will degenerate into four-time, in other words, in the diagonal stage (2) the fore and hind feet will not land together. Three-time rhythm will be restored by allowing the horse to stretch his neck forward, and applying driving aid to the hindquarters.

Relaxing and Suppling

Every athlete warms up before the contest, and prepares himself with loosening exercises. This limbering and warming-up also applies to horses.
After mounting, the rider first walks on a loose rein, then he takes the reins and trots rising, until the initial tension of the horse slackens. Next, cavaletti work will help to establish rhythm, followed by leg-yielding (for lateral suppleness) and upward and downward transitions between trot and canter to loosen the

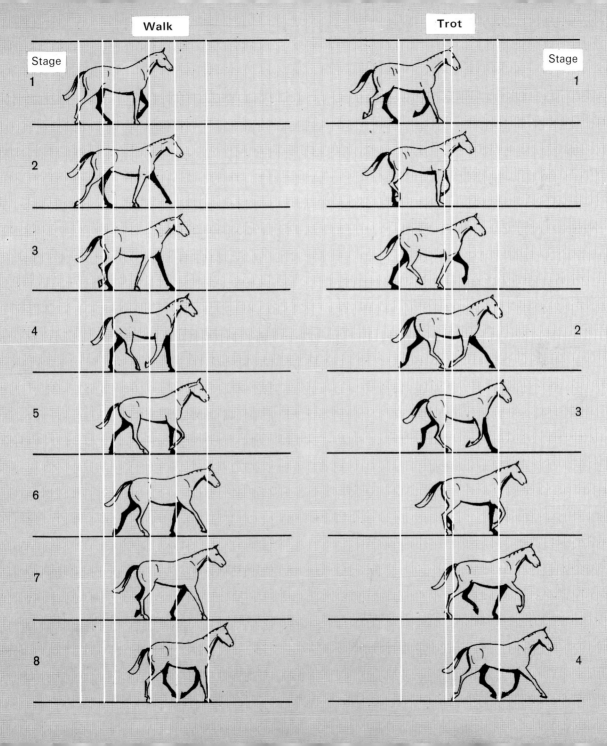

Walk

Stage
1
2
3
4
5
6
7
8

Trot

Stage
1

2

3

4

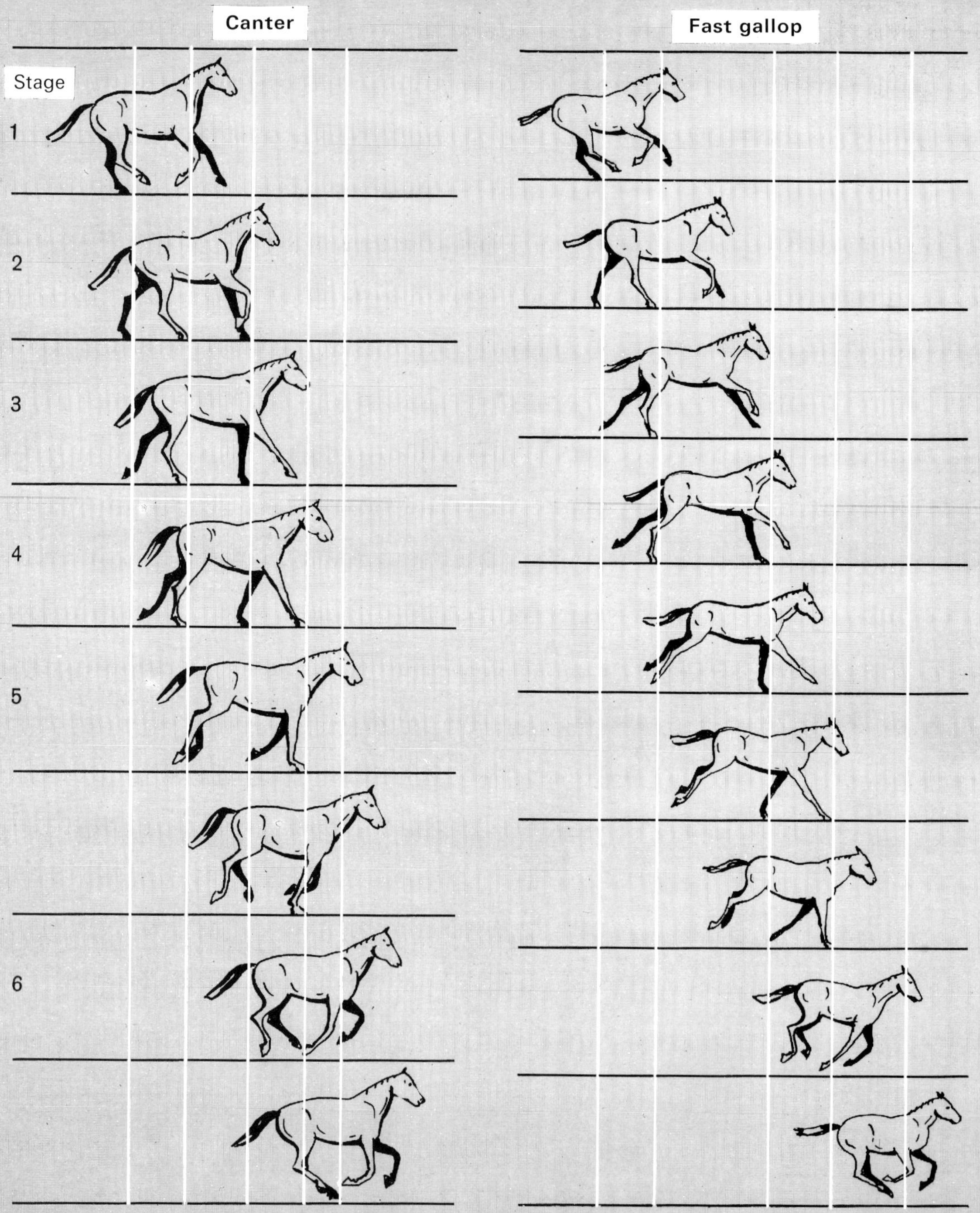

Canter

Fast gallop

Stage

1

2

3

4

5

6

back muscles.
The rider should feel through his seat that the back muscles are no longer taut, since the horse will become far more comfortable to sit on.
After a time the horse will relax the neck muscles, and will look for contact with the rider's hand, by stretching the neck forwards and downwards at the rider's will, when the latter offers the bit by giving the reins; during this movement the horse should maintain the rhythm at all paces constantly, without hurrying. A quiet chewing of the bit will show that all is well in the mouth. True relaxation will be expressed by calm movements, an active back, and a swinging tail, carried neither too high, nor tucked in and 'dead'.

Accepting the Bit

Acceptance means the even and steady contact of the rider's hand with the horse's mouth through the reins. It is through continuous pushing on to this contact from behind that a horse is made to halt 'on the bit'—that is to flex at the poll.
Many riders try to flex the poll without sufficient influence of their legs and seat. The driving aids must work harder than the restraining aids. Acceptance of the bit therefore depends upon the correct balance between the driving and restraining aids; the driving influence must be light, passing through the back and neck into a gentle and sensitive hand, resulting in a willing submission of the horse.

Impulsion

While maintaining the rhythm, the horse must move forward with impulsion. Increased pressure of the seat and thighs will drive the horse forward; the hindquarters must be made to work energetically without hurrying, and with lively steps. Too strong a hand influence will cramp and destroy the thrust from the hindquarters.

When a horse moves freely forward with a relaxed back, the rider will be able to achieve a deep and supple seat.
Changes of tempo within the pace at trot and canter will help to improve impulsion. Speed will be reduced by the use of 'half-halts', which must be carefully controlled to avoid upsetting the balance of the horse.

Straightness

The natural crookedness of the horse must be corrected in schooling. It is said that this crookedness is caused by the position of the embryo in the womb, though this fact has yet to be proved. The crookedness is usually shown when cantering with the off-fore leading, when the horse tends to carry the quarters 'in' to the right, the hind legs not following exactly in the track of the forehand. By riding in curves and circles the horse can be persuaded to yield, and to bend to either side. In executing the circle equally on either rein, the horse can then be ridden straight, on straight lines. If one rides on freshly raked sand, the footmarks of the fore and hind legs can be seen, both on straight lines or in circles, to be following correctly in the same track.

Collection

Collection is created by the response of the horse to the aids to bring the hind legs under the body, while on the move. The horse becomes more 'compact' and as a result, carries the forehand higher. Thus the horse becomes lighter in hand, more mobile, and capable of more supple movements.

These main points of schooling form the basis for work for all classes of dressage—and the rider must master them both in theory and in practice.

Summary

The basic qualities will be produced by the following methods

Quality	Method	Test
Rhythm	■ Correct footfall in the basic paces ■ Cavaletti work ■ Free forward movement ■ Half-halts	Response to the aids to go forward
Relaxation and suppleness	■ Rising trot ■ Leg-yielding ■ Alternate trot and canter ■ Cavaletti work ■ Lungeing ■ Free jumping ■ Work up and down hill	Stretching the neck and 'looking for the bit'; chewing the bit
Accepting the bit	■ Changes of tempo ■ Rein aids—accepting, yielding, steadiness of head	Continuous even contact with the horse's mouth
Impulsion	■ Changes of tempo ■ Transitions ■ Medium trot and canter ■ Increased influence of the aids to keep horse between hand and leg	The hindquarters swing and begin to carry more weight; the rider goes with the movement and is carried along
Straightening	■ Riding in circles ■ Riding turns ■ Change of tempo ■ Lateral work ■ Lungeing	The hindquarters swing, both hind legs carry equal weight; on both curved and straight lines the footprints are equidistant from a median line
Collection	■ Changes of tempo ■ Transitions ■ Half- and full-halts ■ Lateral work ■ Work in hand	Hindquarters work correctly and bear weight; profile and acceptance of the bit constant and steady

Application and Effect of the Leg Aids

Moving Forward	*Moving Sideways*	*General Control*
To create forward movement—in transitions from halt to movement—for increase of tempo—activation of the hindquarters—impulsion—collection; the leg is applied near the girth, the forward edge of the boot should be at the rear edge of the girth; both legs are applied together—for example, for medium or extended trot; leg applied on one side—shoulder-in	The leg maintains the bend of the horse's spine—controls the quarters in small circles and pirouettes and creates forward movement at the completion of the turn	Keeps the horse continuously straight

Application and Effect of the Weight Aids

Weighting Centrally	*Weighting One Side*	*No Weighting*
Only when driving forwards (for example—increase of speed—half-halts—maintenance of impulsion—activation of hindquarters for collection—piaffer and passage with extreme collection)	Canter strike off—turns—lateral work—pirouettes	Relaxation—rising trot—alternate weighting and lightening in the early stages of learning the aids—riding with a light seat—jumping seat

Application and Effect of the Rein Aids

Rein Aids	*Half-Halts*	*Halts*
1. Giving Lengthening the frame Medium and extended paces Interplay of giving and taking, in halts and half-halts **2. Taking** See half-halts **3. Holding** Even and continuous contact between hand and horse's mouth; improvement of paces by increased impulsion, into a softly restraining hand **4. Opposing** Control of turns, maintenance of bend to right or left	■ Control of rhythm ■ Downward transitions ■ Change of tempo ■ Adjustment of balance ■ Preparation for new movement ■ Reining back ■ Alternate rein-back and forward movements	Halts from any pace

Dressage

The Horse

The rider who has used Novice and Elementary dressage tests as the foundation for schooling his horse would do well to consider the aptitude of the animal for further training in dressage. There are clear requirements in conformation to be met:
- A fine head
- Neck well set on
- Shoulders long and sloping
- Withers prominent
- Back not too short, hindquarters not high.

As nothing is ever perfect, even the best horse has defects and weaknesses which must be carefully assessed against its merits. The performance of a dressage horse is dependent not only on conformation, but also on character and temperament. Conformation will show the horse's muscular ability, energy and toughness, but the character and temperament include the inner qualities of courage, intelligence, obedience and willingness to submit to the rider. The ideal horse for dressage is the well-bred thoroughbred or three-quarter bred, in which beauty and natural impulsion abound, provided always that there are no faults of gait.

The Rider

The first essential in the training of the rider is the attainment of a correct seat—supple, upright and deep in the saddle, in order to give the aids correctly, without disturbing the balance of the horse even in the most difficult exercises.

Only thus can the rider achieve understanding and unity with the horse and present a harmonious and pleasing appearance.

The success of a rider depends upon three principles:

1. Ability to master and understand the minds of different horses
2. Sensitive and sympathetic feeling
3. Acquisition of the necessary physical skills.

The first quality is more easily acquired than the other two, which will require years of training. The ability to acquire physical skill varies with different individuals, but it is worth considering that the gymnastic training of the rider should receive more attention in the future.

The rider who aspires to success must put himself in the hands of his trainer, or model himself upon great performers, and follow the path to the end. Success will only come after long and hard endeavour.

Principles of Dressage Training—from Elementary to Medium or Advanced Standard

First stage:
'Coarse' control

Horse

1. Attain and maintain a suitable degree of collection for longer periods of work
2. Improvement of the purity of the rhythm, paces, impulsion and obedience
3. Aim—impulsion, collection, suppleness

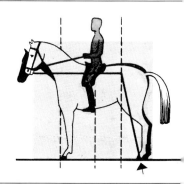

Second stage:
'Fine' control

Horse

1. Learning movements of medium and advanced tests
2. Increased engagement of the hindquarters, bending of the hocks, improving lightness of the forehand
3. Aim—accurate execution of the school figures

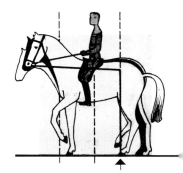

Third stage:
'Precision' control

Horse

1. Consolidation and refinement of advanced exercises at advanced standard including piaffer
2. Testing and correcting weak points
3. Aim—execution of complete tests at advanced level

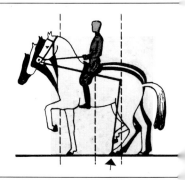

Rider	New exercises	Revision
Improvement in the application of the aids	■ Smaller circles ■ Increasing the circle ■ Travers ■ Renvers ■ Half-pass ■ Half-pirouettes ■ Flying changes	■ Relaxing exercises ■ Changes of tempo ■ Transitions ■ Halts ■ Rein-back ■ Walk pirouettes ■ Counter-canter
Rider Thorough familiarity with the new exercises	■ Half-pass variations (trot and canter) ■ Flying changes to two-time ■ Full pirouettes ■ Work in hand	■ Relaxing exercises ■ Changes of tempo ■ Transitions ■ Halts ■ Rein-back ■ Walk pirouettes ■ Counter-canter
Rider The most refined mastery of the aids	■ Attainment of maximum suppleness ■ One-time flying changes ■ Half-pass zigzag at canter ■ Piaffer ■ Passage	■ Work in hand ■ Flying changes ■ Pirouettes

Dressage Training

Daily work is composed of schooling periods of varying length:

1. *Relaxation phase*—the period of preparation
2. *Working phase*—the main period, including tests of progress
3. *Recovery phase*—the closing period.

Each phase has a clearly defined object, and should be carried out to a careful plan. At the end of the work period the horse should not be overtired, but should be still full of impulsion in all paces. Schooling is based upon the theoretical knowledge of the rider; each phase will only be successful if the rider knows what he is doing and why, and applies this knowledge to the physical and mental ability of his horse. That is to say, he must not only know the anatomy of the horse and the function of the muscles and joints, but must also be able to picture the feelings and understand the reactions of his horse.

The Relaxation Phase. The loosening phase is a recapitulation of the early basic schooling of the horse. The level of training determines the time needed for relaxation but will vary greatly with different horses. Relaxation before work is created by walking, trotting and cantering. Ten to fifteen minutes walking with full extension of the neck is the normal rule, relaxing not only the body but also the mind of the horse. After the walk, start with rising trot. This exercise will only achieve its object if the horse works in calm, regular rhythm. However, should the hindquarters begin to 'drag' and become inactive, impulsion must be created by riding forwards more strongly; but this action must not create tension, as is often the case in strong forward movement; regular rhythm and light contact must be maintained. If using a school or arena, the rider should not simply ride round the track, but should vary the work by circles and changes of rein. Frequent changes of direction will improve the balance of the horse, the engagement of the hindquarters and consequently the impulsion. Transitions between trot and canter in the circle will relax the horse's back and sharpen his reactions to the aids. Again the effect of loosening exercises varies with different horses—some relax better at the canter, in cavaletti work, or on the lunge.

The Work and Test Phase. The rider will pass on to the work phase when he feels the horse to be fully relaxed—the back supple, the impulsion coming from behind, and being accepted softly and steadily in the mouth. After a short break at the walk, the horse should be 'put to the aids'—that is, brought on to the bit, the degree of collection attempted depending on the level of schooling.

Riding with the Double-bridle

The dressage rider has the choice of two types of bit— the snaffle, and the double-bridle, which includes a curb bit.

The horse is ready for the double-bridle when he goes freely forward, accepting the bit willingly in both forward and lateral movements, with no loss of impulsion.

After a rest day, the young horse should always be worked in the snaffle, which should play a major role in schooling at lower levels. The advanced horse will always be ridden in the double-bridle in tests, its stronger effect allowing the rider the greatest degree of control. It is essential, however, that the curb be correctly adjusted, the effect of the bit being dependent upon the height of the port, and the proportions of the upper and lower cheeks. (The longer the lower cheek, the stronger the bit.) It goes without saying that the bit must be exactly the correct

width for the horse's mouth. A higher port means a stronger bit; a small port should be used for sensitive horses, though care should be taken to see that the tongue is not pinched. Lastly, the adjustment of the curb chain affects the strength of the bit; the chain should lie flat in the curb-groove at the back of the lower jaw. Faulty use of the curb is sure to lead to evasions, stiffening and cramping of the paces. If these occur, the rider must revert to the snaffle.
A particular point to watch is that in turns and circles the outer cheek of the curb does not pinch (probably causing tilting of the head).
The work phase is divided into the following parts:

■ Repetition, consolidation, and polishing of previous work
■ New exercises
■ Improvement in muscular ability
■ Testing the level of performance.

There is no rigid theoretical pattern in the work phase,

which must be planned and executed to suit each particular lesson. Work naturally progresses from the easy to the difficult; each lesson must show positive progress, without stagnation. The rider must keep a constant balance between the load of work put on the horse, and the recovery phase. Movements not requiring impulsion, such as halts, rein-back and short turns, can be used in the recovery phase, and yet demand obedience. If difficulties or resistances are met, these must be dealt with before going further into the programme.

The Recovery Phase. The last period of each lesson will be devoted to recovery—ten to fifteen minutes riding on a long rein, or leading with a loosened girth. This 'running down' should *not* take place in the school or manège. Riding out or hacking across country is also a valuable relaxation, and can provide a good opportunity for both work and recovery.

Lunge Work

Lungeing is an important and basic element in schooling, and performs various different functions:

1. **Exercising the Horse.** The horse on the lunge gains confidence, settles down, develops balance and rhythm; the back becomes active, and the horse submits to the shaping action of the side-reins.

2. **Lungeing for Schooling.** With this type of lungeing the rider can positively improve the horse. Horses which are stiff in the back, and therefore have difficulty in flexing to the bridle, will benefit greatly by being lunged before riding. Correct lungeing makes heavy demands on the trainer, who must be able to observe minute differences in the horse's movement and carriage and must be in complete command through the application of the aids of voice, rein and whip.

Aids for Lungeing. With horses that are inclined to go above the bit, one attaches the side-rein lower down on the girth—and vice versa.

The length of the side-reins will be normally equal, with young horses. The inside rein can sometimes be shortened but *never* the outer. If the inner rein is shortened too much the head will be pulled in to the circle, and the quarters will fall out.

With horses which are 'gassy' and wild on the lunge, the side-reins can be further shortened temporarily; when the horse settles and goes forward at the trainer's command the reins can be lengthened again. The natural profile of the horse, with the line of face in front of the vertical, determines the correct length of the side-reins. Once the combination of horse, trainer, lunge, whip and side-reins has reached a satisfactory rhythmical forward movement, changes of tempo and transitions between gaits can be introduced. The interaction of driving and restraining aids and halts will collect the horse, and cause active use of the muscles. Reducing the size of the circle will demand greater collection; but this practice must be discontinued if the purity of pace is lost, through stiffness. The horse, by falling out with the hindquarters, will evade the engagement of the hindquarters, and the lateral bend. At the end of lungeing, a recovery period at the walk must be included.

Faults and Correction

- Insufficient contact
- Tension
- Incorrect footfall
- Horse's neck overbent, face behind the vertical.

A circular swinging of the lunge-rein with simultaneous application of the whip will drive the horse more or further forward. In attempting too much impulsion or collection, rhythm can be lost, as also with efforts to increase the tempo, when the horse may hurry without lengthening the stride.

'More forwards' is a better cure than more collection.

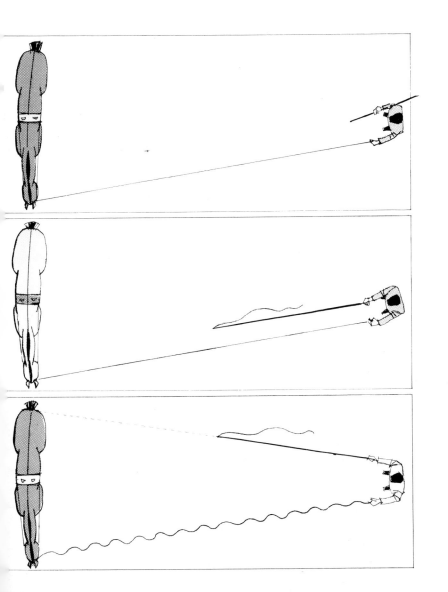

Lungeing without the use of the whip

Use of the whip directed at the horse's shoulder to widen the circle

Half-halt by shortening the rein and applying the whip, to widen the circle

Work in Hand

Work in hand is a useful addition to schooling and, correctly executed, has many advantages.

The rider learns to refine the sensitivity of his hands and gets a feeling for correct collection.

The horse, yielding at the poll, learns to lower his quarters, thus lightening the forehand, and allowing himself to be collected in rhythmic steps. The hocks, deeply flexed, carry more of the weight and allow the paces to become more elevated, leading eventually to the piaffer. However, the piaffer, expression of the greatest impulsion, and lightest forehand, can only be perfected under the rider.

Aids for Work in Hand.

Work in hand is carried out according to the level of schooling of the horse. With the young horse, the work gives him confidence in the trainer, makes him familiar with the dressage whip, and increases his response to the aids.

One begins with the crossing-over of the hindlegs—a movement which loosens the muscles, and compels obedience to the aid. The horse is suppled laterally by the crossing of the hindlegs, and the inward bend at the poll. This exercise should be carried out in the middle of the school, where the horse has more freedom of movement. As with lungeing, one starts on the left rein. The rider, standing by the shoulder, holds the inner snaffle ring with the left hand, walks backwards and leads the horse forward. The forward movement is assisted by clicking the tongue, and by a dressage whip of about 1.20m (4 feet) in length, held in the right hand. The horse is touched carefully with the whip, first just above the fetlock, and later in the region of the girth. The horse, as a result, steps in the arc of a volte (circle of 6m—$19\frac{1}{2}$ feet). If he crosses his hindlegs willingly without tension, the circle can be made still smaller. If the horse yields at the poll, let him follow the hand forward, and at the same time flex the poll.

Next the rider can begin the work in hand proper. The principles of schooling apply to both young and older horses; only the standards set will vary. Work in hand before riding will loosen-up the horse; after riding it will only be used if difficulties have arisen during the riding period.

It is better if on certain days of the week work in hand is carried out some hours after the normal riding period.

[*Translator's note:* The illustration opposite shows two exercises in hand, crossing the hindlegs and piaffer. The author does not mention in the text the method of holding the snaffle reins—the outside rein passing over the neck, and through the inside snaffle ring. The author, without further explanation, embarks on a description of collection and piaffer in hand.]

The horse, allowed to carry the face in front of the vertical, is led forward out of the volte by the rider walking backwards opposite the shoulder. With the aid of whip and voice the

Work in hand crossing over the hindlegs

Piaffer in hand. Hold the snaffle only, not the curb

horse is trotted and walked with short steps, halted several times, then rewarded. The whip is applied below the fetlock—later, a click of the tongue, and a mere hint of the whip should suffice; the need for a strong whip aid indicates a lack of impulsion. If the short steps are successful, the horse can be moved on with the rein aid to a more energetic gait.

Soon, according to the temperament and ability of the horse, some elevated steps can be demanded. At first steps covering less ground but with more energy will be sufficient. If the work has been successful, the horse will begin to respond to the click of the tongue only.

At this point the trainer should think about working on either hand, and the moment has also come to weight the horse with a rider, sitting passively and lightly in the saddle. As schooling progresses, the aids of rein and leg are passed over to the rider, the trainer's whip only being used in support when required.

Faults and Correction. If the horse tries to rush away on the transition from the walk to the trot, restraining rein aids must introduce the walk once more. If the horse goes crooked by bringing the quarters in, the trainer brings the shoulder away from the wall to restore straightness. If the horse comes in with the forehand in order to evade the engagement of the hindquarters, the leading hand is stretched in order to put pressure on the cheek. Irregular steps must be corrected by trotting forwards immediately. Constant application of the whip without forward movement will result in a tense back and irregular steps, and in piaffer the feet will stick to the ground.

At all times, if irregularities appear in the paces, further work must be suspended until the true rhythm is regained.

Schooling for a Medium Test (Class M)

If a rider has schooled his horse up to Elementary Standard (Class L) then he will undoubtedly wish for further progress. It will not be easy to find a Medium or Advanced horse as a schoolmaster, so he must acquire the theoretical and practical knowledge by work which leads on to the new standard.

Foundations for Medium Dressage

The following qualities are the minimum required for this standard:

. *Collection.* The hindquarters, which are increasingly engaged, in order to carry more weight, begin to be lowered, so that the rider feels as if the horse is higher in front.

. *Straightness, suppleness, impulsion,* and *pure rhythm* are essential. The horse must remain constantly on the bit.

. The correct bend of the spine will be expressed in *lateral work,* in the *half-passes,* and in the true and counter-canter in corners or serpentines. In collected canter the three-time rhythm must be maintained.

. In *simple* and *flying changes at the canter* the horse must be straight, and the changes ridden forward.

Travers and *Renvers* are no longer required in the new dressage tests at this level: nevertheless, they are of great value in schooling as they improve the gymnastic ability of the horse, increasing balance, collection and obedience.
Collection will be the highest priority for all further schooling, for it improves the balance, acceptance of the bit, and the paces, and compels obedience in the horse. Only by achieving collection from behind does the horse engage the hindquarters, rounding the back and lightening the forehand.
In a test the horse must move freely, full of impulsion, being steady on the bit and responding accurately to the aids.

Lateral Work

Lateral work will make the horse more agile and more supple. It should only be started when the horse, working in circles and voltes, has learnt to flex the inside hock more strongly.
The execution of lateral work at the walk is valuable only for the reason that it makes the horse familiar with the aids; work at the walk will not be of much gymnastic value.

[*Translator's note:* The author now describes two lateral movements— *Schultervor* and *Schulterherein*— literally, shoulder-forward and shoulder-in. The nearest equivalent in English to the former is 'position right (or left)'.
In the diagram on the opposite page, the author shows 'shoulder-forward' with the forelegs brought slightly in from the track, the horse bent to the left, and the hindquarters remaining straight. Other German authorities (notably Müseler in *Riding Logic*) show 'position left' with both the quarters and the forehand bent inwards round the rider's inside leg. I have always used Brandl's version as 'position right or left' and propose, therefore, to use the term in translation here.]

Position Right or Left. The introduction to lateral work is through this movement, on a single track. For horses which have not yet achieved much collection the sideways displacement of the tracks is minimal, in order to make the movement easy for the horse. On the long side of the school, the horse is positioned with the inner hindleg stepping towards a point between the front feet, and the outer hindleg follows the front foot on the same side. The horse is bent inwards equally through the whole length (in this case to the left). If the quarters fall out the bend would be lost. The aids are similar to the shoulder-in, but demand a lesser degree of bend. Position right or left is best ridden after coming out of the corner on to the long side. Keeping the bend, the forehand is led in by both reins to the inner edge of the track; the inside rein demands the bend and the degree of displacement of the shoulder, the outer rein limits the bend, and controls the tempo. The rider's inside leg, applied behind the girth, should maintain the bend of the

horse's ribs, stimulate the activity of the horse's inside leg, and cause the slight sideways movement. The rider's outside leg contains the quarters and assists the forward motion. The rider adapts his seat to the bend of the horse, keeping his hips parallel to those of the horse.

Shoulder-in. This is the basic lateral exercise out of which all others are developed. It differs from 'position right or left' in that the horse is more bent, and the forehand is placed further in from the track, increasing the angle of attack.
The horse now moves in such a way that both his inside legs step in front of the outside pair, with the head bent away from the direction of movement, and the outer shoulder on the same track as the inner hip.
Important: the rider's weight must rest on the inner seat-bone. At first only demand a few steps, then go straight on and pick up the impulsion.
The shoulder-in can also be

ridden on the centre line, on either rein.

Faults and Correction. The main fault is too strong a use of the inside rein, causing too much bend of the neck, and the outer shoulder then falls out. As a correction, strengthen the outside rein and drive forward with the outside leg. Horses which go behind the bit must be driven forward. If irregularities in the rhythm begin to develop, stop the lateral work at once.

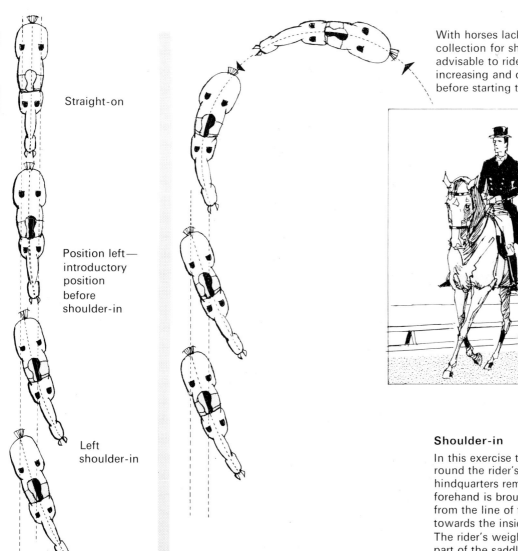

Straight-on

Position left—
introductory
position
before
shoulder-in

Left
shoulder-in

With horses lacking the necessary collection for shoulder-in, it is advisable to ride the exercise of increasing and decreasing the circle before starting the shoulder-in

Shoulder-in

In this exercise the horse is bent round the rider's inside leg. The hindquarters remain in the track, the forehand is brought in half a pace from the line of the outer hindleg, towards the inside of the track.
The rider's weight should rest on the part of the saddle shown in black in the illustration

Medium walk   Extended walk   Collected walk

Collected trot   Medium trot   Extended trot

Collected canter   Medium canter   Extended canter

The diagram on the opposite page illustrates the difference between the collected, medium and extended paces in the different gaits.

Reining Back

In the alternate backward and forward movements required in advanced tests, the transitions between forward and backward must be fluent and free. The hindlegs are not brought square, as in the halt, but the change is achieved by moving the legs immediately backwards or forwards

Reducing and Enlarging the Circle

In this exercise the horse is bent at the poll and in the spine to conform to the curve of the circle; the rider must bring his outer shoulder slightly forward, in order that his seat may conform to the direction of movement.

The circle is reduced by riding with the quarters in, and increased by pushing outwards in the style of shoulder-in or leg-yielding

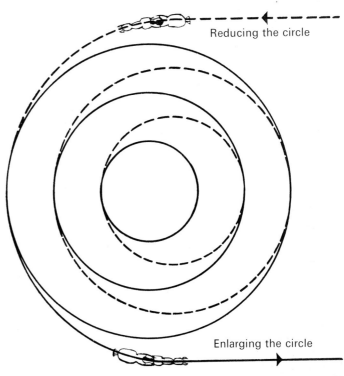

Reducing the circle

Enlarging the circle

Travers

This is a lateral movement in which the quarters are brought inwards, and the horse bent in the direction of movement. The track of the outer hindleg is at least half a pace inside that of the outer foreleg. The outside legs step forwards and sideways over the inside pair. Travers can be ridden in walk, trot or canter.

Execution and Aids. Before the transition to travers, the horse must be collected, without losing the forward movement. As the rider comes out of the corner, when the horse's head nearly reaches the wall of the long side, he gives a half-halt, and begins the travers.

The rider's outside leg acts on the hindquarters in the same rhythm and the outer hindleg is being raised. The angle should be only sufficient to bring the outer hindleg on to the same track as the inner foreleg.

The horse is bent round the rider's inside leg, which maintains the forward movement, and prevents the quarters from travelling too far to the side.

The inside rein positions the horse, and leads it forward; the outside rein limits the bend. To straighten the horse, drive forward with both legs, the inside leg being stronger.

Faults and Correction. The most common fault is to bend the horse's neck at the shoulders, and to position the quarters at too wide an angle. The outer hindleg then moves more sideways than forwards, and does not carry enough weight.

Increased use of the inside leg and the outside rein will restore the correct bend. An excellent means of increasing the horse's obedience is to make transitions from one lateral movement to another—for example, shoulder-in, followed by a volte, and then travers, the bend remaining unchanged.

Straight on

Introductory position to the exercise (quarters-in)

The angle can be increased as the horse becomes more supple; but the hindleg should not be brought in more than one full pace from the original track

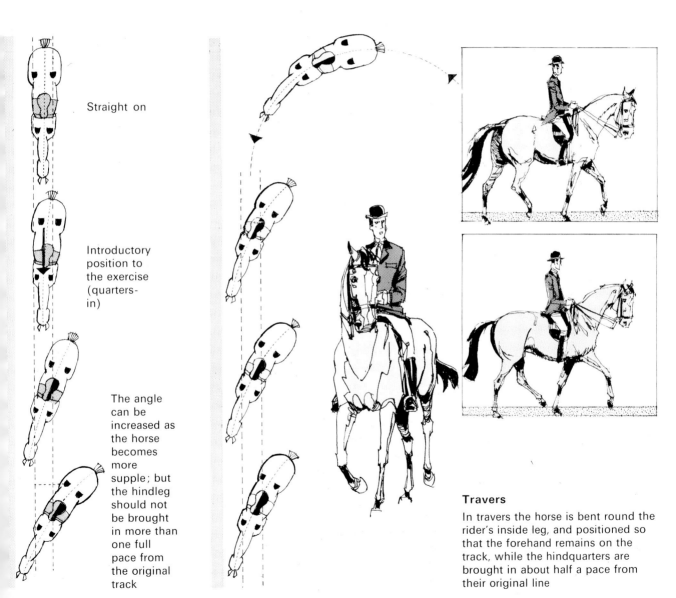

Travers

In travers the horse is bent round the rider's inside leg, and positioned so that the forehand remains on the track, while the hindquarters are brought in about half a pace from their original line

Renvers

The renvers plays a similar part to the travers in the schooling of the horse, but is a more difficult exercise. In this movement, the forehand is brought in from the track, at least half a pace from the line of the inner hindleg. The horse is bent in the direction of movement, and the outside legs step in front of and over the inside pair. The renvers can be ridden at walk, trot or canter.

[*Translator's note:* The term 'outside' and 'inside' leg of either horse or rider always refers to the bend of the horse—the concave side being the inside, the convex the outside— regardless of the position of the horse relative to the wall of the school or arena.]

Execution and Aids. The position of the renvers is created by the rider's outside leg, in conjunction with the inside rein, which establish the bend of the horse round the rider's inside leg, which maintains the forward drive. The outer rein, lying against the neck, determines the degree of bend, and regulates the tempo. At the end of the renvers, the forehand is brought back straight in front of the hindquarters. The rider must be careful not to twist the upper part of the body, or to collapse the hip, but must sit upright, and keep his own shoulders parallel to the horse's shoulders.

Faults and Correction. If the rider's inside leg drives too strongly the horse will run on to the hand; the aids must be carefully co-ordinated. Too much lateral work may reduce the impulsion. If the horse evades by being behind the bit, or by striking off into canter, then the rider must ride forward, keeping the horse's shoulder in position right or left, until he comes back to the trot, and can be prepared again for the lateral movement.
For ease of movement the renvers is normally ridden out of a half-pirouette, made somewhat larger than usual, so that forward movement is maintained. A few steps of renvers will be enough at first; the aim of the exercise is increased activity of the hindquarters, supple bend of the spine and obedience to the leg aid.

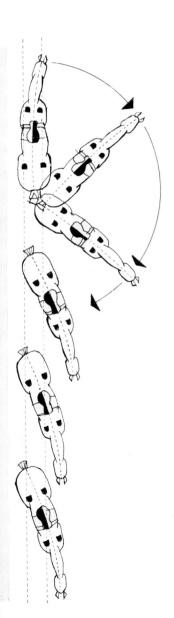

Renvers

Renvers is the opposite movement to travers, though the aids are similar. The horse goes with bend in the direction of movement, the forehand at least half a pace in from the track of the inside hindleg

The Half-pass

The half-pass is a diagonal movement, usually towards the long side or the centre-line of the school.

The horse is bent towards the direction of movement, the forehand always slightly preceding the hindquarters.

[*Translator's note:* In the diagram opposite the horse's quarters are shown slightly leading—a fault.]

The movement increases the freedom of the shoulder, and improves suppleness, balance, and impulsion. (Half-passes can be ridden at walk, trot or canter.)

Execution and Aids. Half-passes are first ridden in collected trot, and started from a half-volte. At the end of the half-volte, the outside rein, supported by the inner, checks the circling movement —the horse is then led back diagonally to the side of the school. The rider's outside leg, behind the girth, causes the sideways movement. The bend should be through the whole length of the horse, the position of the horse's head not bent more than the rest of the neck. The rider's weight is to the side towards the movement. The rider increases the length of the movement by riding on to the centre-line at the end of the school, and beginning his half-pass back to the track after one horse's length straight.

This prevents the forehand from falling in and the horse running away from the aids. The rider must also prevent the quarters from leading. The outside rein limits the degree of bend, and supports the inside rein in keeping the forward movement.

Faults and Correction. An exaggerated head position (too much bend at the poll) cramps the gait and leads to faults of rhythm and insufficient collection. At the change of rein in the counter-change of hand (zigzag), the horse must be straightened, otherwise the quarters will lead in the new direction: the rider must sit upright; if he collapses a hip, or sits against the direction of movement (a common fault in young riders) the horse will lose balance.

Half-pass

Half-pass to the left

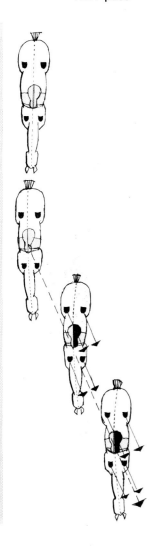

Canter half-pass

10   9   8   7   6

Flying Changes at the Canter

The flying change is demanded at Medium and Advanced levels. The canter consists of three footfalls, and a period of suspension; the change must be made during the period of suspension. The change must be ridden forwards without checking, straight, with no swinging of the quarters, and changes from right to left or vice versa must be similar. The horse must be well balanced and moving freely forward in canter; on no account should changes be attempted before the rest of the horse's schooling is well up to standard.

It is, as a rule, easier to start with the change from right lead to left lead. At the end of the long side, turn back in a small half-circle, and after a few strides straight push the horse sideways with the outside leg and seat-bone back towards the track. On reaching the track the change is made by applying the right leg behind the girth. If the change is made, break off the exercise and rest at the walk on a long rein.

For the next week's work it is as well to consolidate this one change only, before attempting the change from left to right. As the horse improves in fluency, the rider will no longer need the sideways movement before the change, but will gradually ride the horse more forward, in order to achieve a straight change. The rider must be careful not to collapse the hip during the aid for the change. Setbacks are certain to occur during schooling; it is therefore all the more important not to begin work on the changes until the horse is ready for it.

The basic preparation begins by frequently striking off into canter from the walk, on both reins. The canter from the walk and walk from canter without trot strides must be carried out correctly and straight on both reins. When beginning the flying changes the rider must choose the method which suits his horse the best. The counter-canter also provides good preparation; the suppling effect of this exercise will be a great help to the horse's balance.

Execution and Aids. In the counter-canter, the changes are best made at the following places in the school:
In the middle of the short side, or crossing the centre-line in the 20 m (65 feet) circle; later at any point of the circle. After the circle exercises, the

5   4   3   2   1

flying change is ridden on a straight line against the wall, from the outside lead to the inside; then from inside to out against the wall. When the changes are fluent and straight, they may be ridden on the centre-line; finally in serpentines in the whole arena. The aids for the change are the same as the canter strike off. In changing from counter to true lead, the rider's inside leg is taken forward on the girth, and the outside leg is applied behind the girth. The horse's head is positioned slightly inward, and the rider's weight transferred from outside to inside. The rider's inside leg on the girth demands the change. All three applications of the aid take place at the same time.

Faults and Correction. Horses which change in front

and are 'late behind' (or sometimes the other way round), or which do not come through with the hindlegs, must first be improved at the canter.

Crookedness at the change must be corrected by riding more forward. Changes which gain too little ground, or changes with too high a croup, must be corrected by a half-halt followed by aids driving forward. The more supple the horse, the more confident and reponsive to the rider's aids will he become. Changes in three, two and one-time can only be attempted when the horse has really mastered the single change.

Advanced Dressage

Advanced tests make the highest demands on the

gymnastic ability of the horse. Very hard work will be necessary, far beyond the requirement of Medium Standard, which should have been thoroughly mastered. A horse which is not well-rounded, or very well co-ordinated, cannot hope to compete.

Flying Changes, up to One-time

Once the single change is mastered, changes every third stride may be attempted.

Execution and Aids. The best way to teach changes in a straight line is on the long side of the school, where the wall or boards prevent the quarters swinging out; a slight

inward bend with the inside rein will prevent the quarters swinging in.

It is common experience to find that intelligent horses will anticipate the rider's aids in making 'tempo changes'. The only cure is to break off the exercise at once, and to return to single changes.

In the early schooling stages, the rider's aim was to teach the aids, and to obtain the change by any means. Now the changes must be perfected, ridden more fluently, and in a perfect straight line.

Once the horse can carry out two-time changes, with a supple and light self-carriage, the one-time changes can be taught.

At first two changes will be enough—from the true canter to the counter-lead and back again. Frequent patting and rest at the walk should reward success. Increasing numbers of changes can then be put together.

Faults and Correction.

Inexperienced riders often unbalance the horse by giving the aids too late; or give the aids too strongly, or take the lower leg too far back. Another fault is throwing the weight of the upper body from side to side, or exaggerating the bend of the horse's neck in position right or left. This kind of aid makes the horse crooked, and throws him off balance. Incomplete changes behind are often the result of overworking the horse in flying changes.

One-time changes

Flying changes in four-time

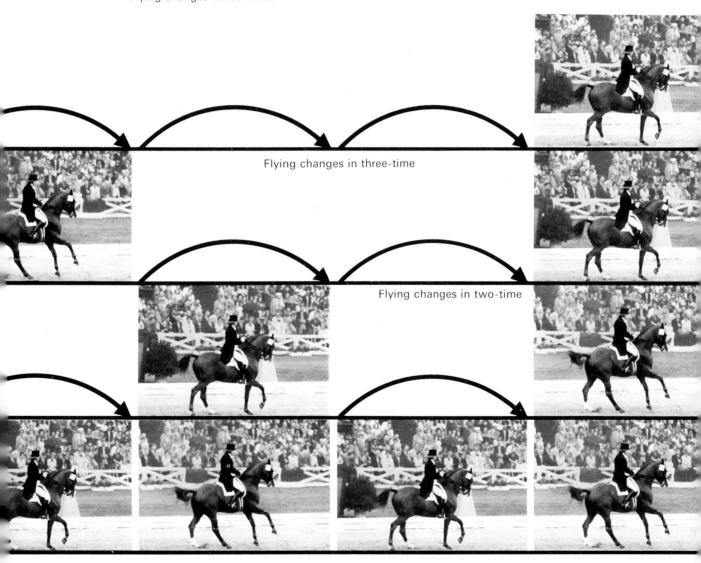

Flying changes in three-time

Flying changes in two-time

Canter Pirouettes

The pirouette ranks amongst the most difficult exercises of dressage. In the half-pirouette (180°), the horse turns round the hindquarters in three or four strides, in the full pirouette (360°), in six to eight strides; the hindquarters, retaining the correct sequence of footfalls and rhythm, remain on the spot. The inside hindfoot forms the centre of the arc, which the forehand describes.

The pirouette is taught out of a travers or renvers position or, with younger horses, from the half-pass at the canter.

Execution and Aids. In the pirouette the inside rein leads the horse into the turn. The rider's inside leg, lying near the girth, maintains the canter rhythm, and prevents the horse's inner shoulder from falling in. The rider's outside leg is applied behind the girth and prevents the hindquarters from falling out. The outer rein supports the position of the head and neck, which is bent to the inside. The horse must be light on the bit, or the hindquarters cannot be engaged with enough activity. The rider shifts his weight to the inner seat bone, keeping the body upright. At the end of the half or full pirouette the outside rein stops the sideways movement, then the rider's inside leg and seat drive the horse forward again in a straight line.

In the early stages of training for the pirouette, it can be introduced by the half-pass, as in the exercise of reducing the circle, thus retaining the forward movement. The size of the pirouette can be varied at the rider's will.

Faults and Correction. If the hindquarters fall out before or during the pirouette, this will be a bad fault, as will the opposite; that is, if the horse evades the aids by turning too quickly. If the horse turns on the spot, but loses the canter, the pirouette will be judged worse than if the hindlegs describe a larger arc, but the canter remains regular.

It is unwise to attempt too many pirouettes in the search for success—forward impulsion must be restored between times by cantering forward at medium and extended canter, before returning to another pirouette. When a pirouette is demanded at a particular point on a straight line, the movement is begun when the quarters reach that point.

The great difficulty is not to

Frau Liselott Linsenhoff riding Piaff— **Pirouette** to the left. As can be clearly seen from this picture the pirouette requires a horse to have the hocks well engaged. The horse, with quarters lowered, is describing a very small circle, without losing the correct sequence of footfalls lose the impulsion, when the forward movement is checked in order to start the turn. The pirouette requires impulsion and balance, as well as supreme obedience. Its performance provides a good indication of the level of schooling of the horse.

Piaffer

The piaffer is an elevated trot on the spot. The horse's legs are raised diagonally in pairs, in regular rhythm. The toe of the forefoot should be raised about to the middle of the cannon-bone of the other leg, which remains on the ground. The hindleg is raised rather less—to almost the height of the fetlock of the other leg. Balance, steady impulsion and complete obedience are the foundations of a regular piaffer.

Execution and Aids.
Preliminary training will include supple and smooth transitions into and out of collection, and increase of pace. The rider will practise changing tempo on the long side of the school, at the trot, reducing the ground gained more and more.

After a few shortened steps have been obtained, the rider should revert to collected trot. Coming into piaffer the rider must sit deeper in the saddle and increase the pressure on the horse's back by bracing his own back, thus driving the horse more on to the bit. The rider's leg aids, applied on the girth, should drive the horse's quarters under him, and maintain the rhythm. The rider must only take the reins enough to prevent the horse moving forward, without the horse leaning on the hand. The rider must sit absolutely still during the piaffer. An assistant on the ground can support the movement with the whip, as in work in hand.

Faults and Correction. Too much use of the whip easily leads to tension and disobedience. The result will be hurried, irregular steps, as well as a head held too high. With horses that are too strong in hand, or which lack the ability to lower the quarters, the croup will escape upwards, or the hindfeet will stick to the ground. Too deep an engagement of the hindquarters prevents a light lifting of the hindlegs. During schooling the piaffer should always be practised so that the horse tends to move forwards by a small amount.

R

Piaffer

Demonstrated by Herr Kizimov on Ikhor, showing the sequence of footfall in all its phases. Although in this illustration the lowered hindquarters are allowing the shoulder and forelegs to move freely, the lack of activity in the back and mouth combine to prevent a better elevation of the hindlegs

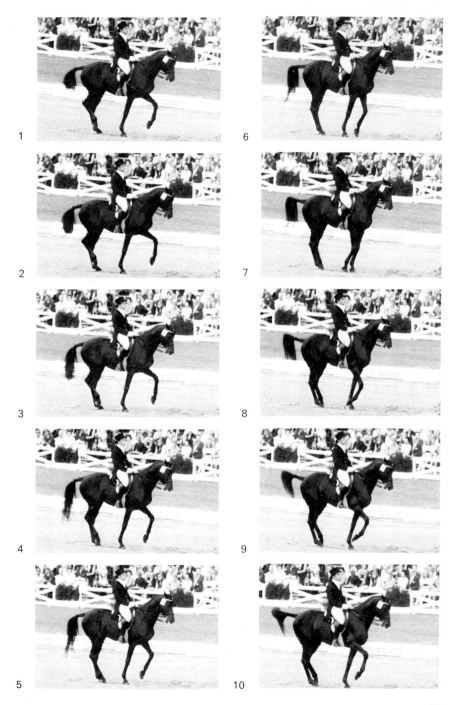

1

2

3

4

5

6

7

8

9

10

Passage

The passage is a floating trot, with a long period of suspension. The horse springs from one diagonal pair of legs to the other, with a longer suspension than in trot. Passage is demanded both in straight lines and in turns and circles.

Execution and Aids. The passage can be taught from the piaffer or from the walk, depending on the horse's muscular ability, temperament, and level of schooling. If a horse has learnt the piaffer well, the passage should be developed out of the piaffer. The passage is taught by changes of tempo following one another in quick succession. The sequence of driving and restraining aids will cause the horse to produce some suspended steps. If the piaffer is less well established, the horse may be taught the passage from the walk.

The aids for the passage are the same as those for the trot. A light hand, supple upright seat, back well braced, and increased influence of the legs will produce the elevated paces. The whip aid is very valuable, applied immediately behind the rider's leg.

Faults and Correction. A faulty passage is one in which the horse raises the forelegs, but only drags the hindlegs along. Another common fault is unevenness of the hindlegs, caused either by the horse being crooked, or by the rider's legs not being used equally on both sides. The best remedy is to ride the horse more forward.

Passage

Frau Linsenhoff on Piaff. The passage, ridden out of a turn, shows Piaff moving with good collection, with hindquarters lowered and hocks well engaged. Impulsion, rhythm and straightness are the hallmarks of a good passage. The energetic movement forwards and upwards allows a smooth transition into the exercise; the rider's seat is supple, hands low, and the aids scarcely visible

Preparation for a Dressage Test

Success in competition will depend on correct and methodical preparation beforehand. The time and manner of 'riding-in' will depend on the character of each individual horse. The rider must think not only about the state of training of the horse, but also about the effect of strange surroundings, and the tensions of the competition atmosphere.

The work is naturally organised in such a way that the horse enters the arena at his best. With temperamental horses it may be wise to do the preliminary work some hours before, and after a rest in the stable, the horse is brought out for a short final period of preparation. With horses lacking in impulsion, it is sensible to retain the freshness, by only riding-in just before the test.

Suppling exercises ensure the willing submission of the whole muscular system.

Obedience exercises consolidate the response to the aids to go forwards, for downward transitions, and for lateral movements.

Collection comes from the lowering and engagement of the hindquarters, and the increased lightening of the forehand.

The rider should not demand, in the riding-in period, more than the standard required in the test, or he may spoil rather than improve the horse. The work should include precise halts, positive move-off, accurate transitions between the paces, and steady rhythm.

The Dressage Test

The following pages (50–55) show the details of a test of Olympic standard. Josef Neckermann, Bronze medallist, demonstrates the different movements during his performance in the 1972 Olympic Games in Munich.

The collective marks at the end of the test are awarded as follows:

1. Paces (freedom and regularity)

2. Impulsion (desire to move forward, elasticity of the steps, suppleness of the back, and engagement of the hindquarters)

3. Submission (attention and confidence; harmony, lightness and ease of the movements; acceptance of the bridle and lightness of the forehand)

4. Rider's position, seat and use of the aids.

To be deducted:

Penalties for exceeding the time (half a point for each commenced second)

Penalties for wrong course or omissions.

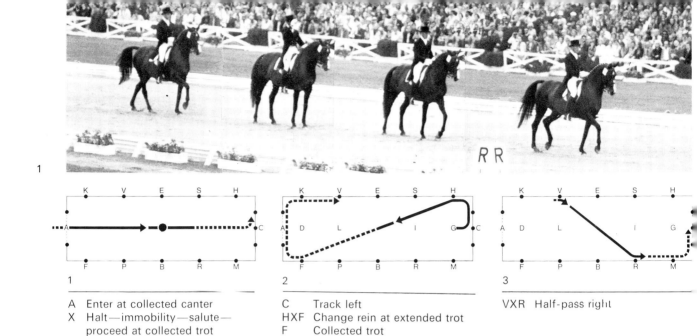

1

A	Enter at collected canter	C	Track left
X	Halt—immobility—salute— proceed at collected trot	HXF	Change rein at extended trot
		F	Collected trot

VXR Half-pass right

2

3

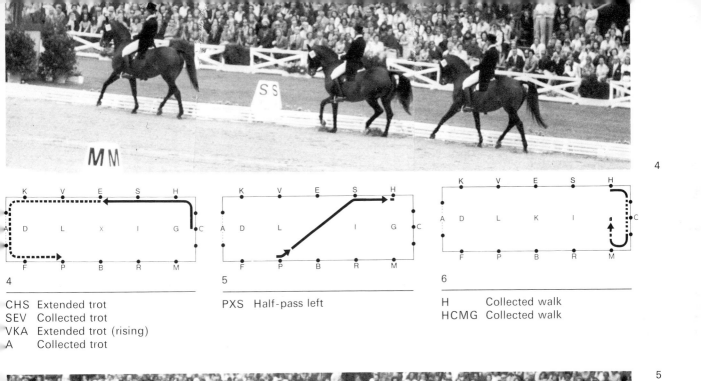

4

4

CHS Extended trot
SEV Collected trot
VKA Extended trot (rising)
A Collected trot

PXS Half-pass left

H Collected walk
HCMG Collected walk

5

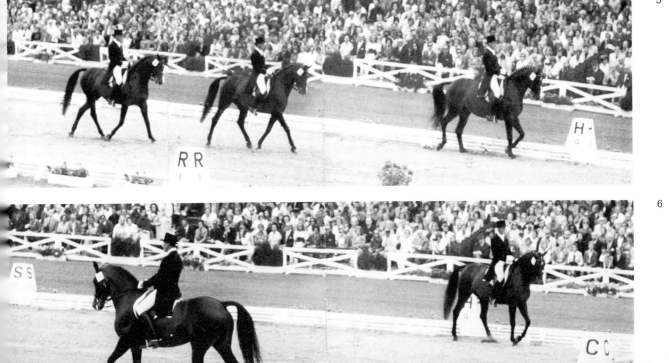

6

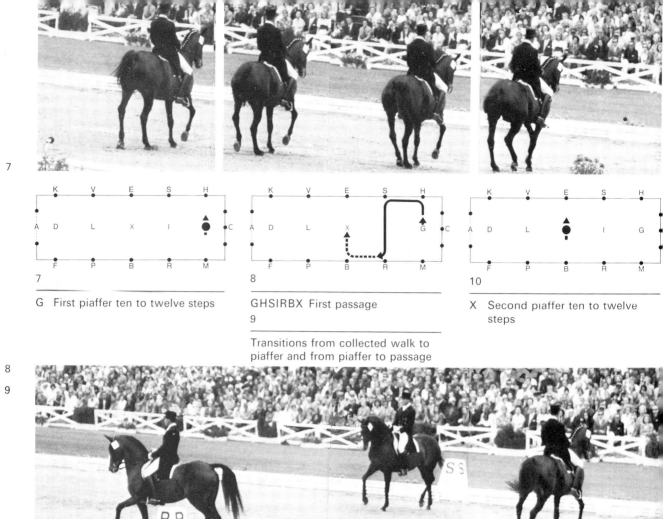

K	V	E	S	H			

7

G   First piaffer ten to twelve steps

8

GHSIRBX   First passage

9

Transitions from collected walk to piaffer and from piaffer to passage

10

X   Second piaffer ten to twelve steps

11

12

13

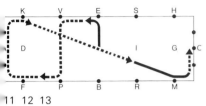
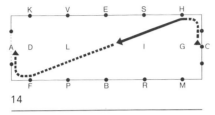
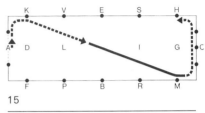

11 12 13

14

15

XEVLPFA	Second passage
A	Extended trot
KXM	Change rein at extended trot
M	Collected trot

C	Medium walk
HXF	Change rein at extended walk
F	Collected walk

A	Collected canter right
KXM	On the diagonal nine changes of leg every second stride (finishing on the left leg)

14

15

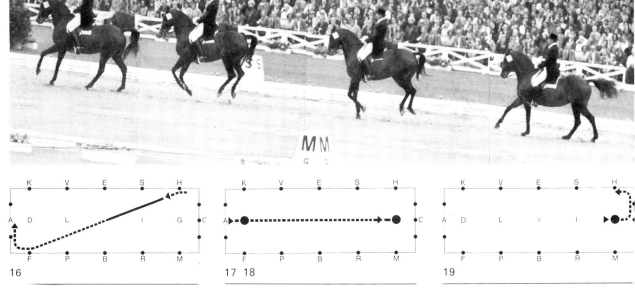

16

16 17 18 19

HXF On the diagonal fifteen changes of leg every stride (finishing on the right leg)

A Down centre line
D Pirouette right, between D and G Nine changes of leg every stride (finishing on the left leg)

G Pirouette left
C Track left

19

19

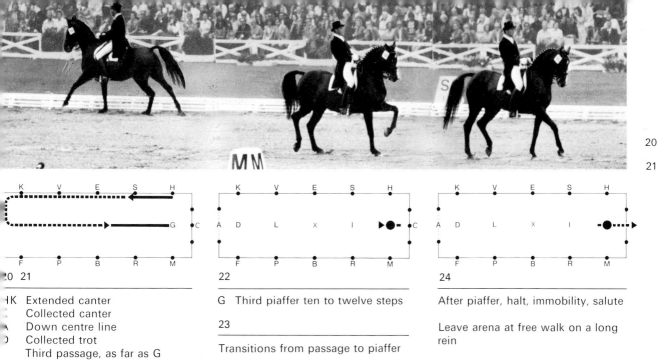

	K	V	E	S	H			K	V	E	S	H			K	V	E	S	H	
								A	D	L	X	I	C		A	D	L	X	I	
	F	P	B	R	M			F	P	B	R	M			F	P	B	R	M	

20 21

22

24

HK Extended canter
 Collected canter
 Down centre line
 Collected trot
 Third passage, as far as G

G Third piaffer ten to twelve steps

23

Transitions from passage to piaffer

After piaffer, halt, immobility, salute

Leave arena at free walk on a long rein

Show-jumping

The Horse

In contrast to the dressage horse, the show-jumper is less limited to a particular conformation, in that the need for good basic paces is not so essential.
Rather one looks for jumping power, in order to get the height over big fences; therefore good muscular development of the whole body is essential. Other positive requirements of conformation are:

- Not too large a head
- Freedom of the jaw
- Not too short a neck
  Long sloping shoulder
  High withers
  A long sloping croup.

Special attention should be given to soundness of limb, and suppleness in movement. When inspecting before buying, always see the horse jumping free, and in practice jumping, both in speed and height.
If the horse lets its legs dangle, or if it does not fold when rapped at the jump, it should not be bought—a horse without talent can rarely be better then mediocre.
A more common horse, calm in temperament, and therefore more submissive, is preferred to the horse with too much breeding. The more blood in the pedigree, the greater the tendency to run on to the rider's hand and to go faster and faster.
Any horse can be taught to jump, if worked carefully and consistently; dressage and gymnastic jumping will produce suppleness. The problem of finding the best horse is less a matter of breeding, than one of conformation, temperament, submission—and above all, the rider must be on top.

The Rider

The rider should not only have a sound knowledge of the basics of riding, enabling him to school his horse, but should also have a good general athletic ability.
He should practise physical training to keep himself in good shape, and should do special exercises to strengthen the muscles used in jumping and dressage. Concentration, determination, and quick reactions are other essential qualities.

The Rider's Seat. The rider needs a supple, flexible seat, enabling him to go with the movement of the horse during the jump. A stable position of the rider's leg, and a light hand, with the horse accepting the bit, will balance the horse on the approach, and at take-off, and will control direction and speed between the fences.

1

2

The Rider's Seat

In jumping, the balance of the rider's height is different from dressage. The hindquarters are unweighted, and free to develop the thrust, instead of

carrying the weight. From this stems the 'forward seat' which has, however, three points in common with the dressage seat: Balance—Suppleness—

7

8

4

5

6

Harmony with the movement. The picture sequence shows one of the best show-jumpers in the world in exemplary style—a supple and light movement of the body, with perfect control. The horse looks relaxed and contented, using his power and skill to the best of his ability.

10

11

12

Show-jumping Training

Principles of Training the Show-jumping Horse

From 'coarse control' to 'fine control'

Principles of Training the Rider

HORSE

RIDER

First stage

1. Suppleness and relaxation during the whole period of daily work
2. Muscular improvement through endurance training
3. Aim—to create suppleness and obedience

1. Perfection of the seat, smooth co-ordination with the movement of the horse
2. Improvement of the aids—on the ground and over jumps
3. Practice of difficult problems
4. Correct assessment of the ability and capacity for work of the jumping horse

Second stage

1. Improvement of obedience, activity, stamina
2. Improvement of technique over single and combination obstacles
3. Aim: improvement of jumping ability

1. Practice over different types of obstacle and course—height and speed—combinations of different distances
2. General improvement of the aids, tactics, etc.
3. Making a training plan

Third stage

1. Perfection of jumping technique
2. Correction of weaknesses
3. Jumping at Grade B or A Standard
4. Improvement of stamina and capacity for work

1. Correction of faults in seat and aids
2. Improved application of the aids
3. Gaining tactical experience
4. Study of relevant literature; making a training plan

NEW LESSONS	REPETITION

First stage

- Gymnastic jumping
- Introducing new fences
- Combinations at different distances
- Jumping on the lunge
- Preparation for special competitions

- Relaxing exercises
- Work on the ground
- Changes of tempo
- Transitions
- Halts and half-halts
- Cavaletti work
- Gymnastic jumping
- Combinations and single jumps
- Cross-country work

Second stage

- Combinations at normal, short and long distances
- Flying changes at canter
- Jumping against the clock

- Suppling exercises
- Work on the ground as above
- Cavaletti work
- Gymnastic and speed jumping

Third stage

- Achievement of complete suppleness
- Change of régime between competitions—rest, periods at grass, lungeing, light exercise and activity training

As above

Faults

- Jerky movements of the rider during the jump disturb the harmony and balance of the movement.
- Stirrups too short inhibit the influence of the seat.
- On landing, the rider fails to restore his balance quickly.

Show-jumping Training

It is assumed that the young horse has the basic schooling behind it, and has already shown above-average ability in Novice and Grade C classes. By now he should have paces that are full of impulsion, and be obedient and straight. After training in dressage, show-jumping and cross-country (or the hunting field), he should be capable of competing calmly and obediently in the ring. Both horse and rider should be physically fit, able to accept the further specialised training and build-up of capacity for work which will take them beyond

The picture series above shows the approach and take-off—on the approach the rider needs the greatest concentration and influence; after take-off his duty is not to interfere with the horse during the jump

Grade B level, and will enable them to maintain that standard in the future.

The training plan will therefore include:

- *Dressage:* continuous work to improve suppleness, obedience and activity
- *Endurance:* training at the canter
- *Jumping:* schooling over all types of obstacle.

Dressage Training

The horse's capacity for achievement will be largely determined by the continual improvement of suppleness, obedience and correctness of the paces. Although dressage will only form one part of the training plan, the work in developing rhythm, impulsion, straightness and collection is necessary to ensure a rapid response to the rider's aids, especially in shortening and lengthening the stride. The horse must learn to go freely, accepting the bit, with active hindquarters. A high degree of collection is not required. The dressage training of a show-jumper is divided into several sections:

1. Improving the general standard of dressage. The aim is a responsive horse, going with natural balance, answering the aids willingly. The rider should not accept less than Advanced Elementary standard, plus the single flying change at the canter.
2. Elimination of weaknesses which come to light in competition. Improvement of the rider's seat and application of the aids. Regaining form lost through staleness.
3. The rider should work to produce a horse which, when ridden with a light jumping seat, responds instantly to increase of speed and to half-halts, and is able to make transitions from extended to collected canter and vice versa, without taking too much hold or resisting the rider's hand.

General Training. This will consist of a combination of dressage and gymnastic jumping. Dressage at Novice and Elementary standard will maintain the correctness of the paces, relaxation, suppleness and obedience. Work on changes of tempo, transitions from one gait to another and work in curves and circles will prepare the horse for jumping training.
If the horse can be ridden in a relaxed, fluent, calm way over fences, and then allows itself to be 'put to the aids' again

afterwards without resistance, the object of this stage will be achieved.

Gymnastic jumping will improve the actual technique over obstacles, and the power and activity of the horse. The gymnastic obstacles should be jumped from the trot at first, until the horse learns to 'jump with its back' (that is, bascule). The distances between the obstacles, and the height and speed, are adjusted to suit the length of stride of each horse. The first jump should always be inviting and lower than the others. If the horse has a tendency to get under his fences, then earlier take-off can be encouraged by the introduction of cavaletti, and the increase of the distances.

1

4

2

5

3

6

7

8

9

10

11

Lack of impulsion, or missing the
take-off stride, can lead to serious
difficulties with fences of this size.
The fault at the first part of the
combination reduces the impulsion,
so that the horse can no longer get
out over the big parallel. The horse
must have a big heart to carry on in
this case

By placing cavaletti behind a
gymnastic obstacle the
stretching of the neck and the
arching of the back will be
improved.
As the horse progresses, the
distances will be shortened to
the minimum, reducing the
length of the stride, and
forcing the horse to fold the
front legs.
Continual jumping without
altering the fences makes the
horse sluggish and
disobedient. Jumping without
previous loosening-up, and
overfacing the horse, soon
lead to tiredness.

Endurance Training

It often happens that horses incur faults in the last third of a show-jumping course, attributable neither to lack of concentration in the rider nor to technical mistakes, but to the loss of power through failure of stamina.

It is wise therefore to include endurance as a part of the jumping training. This training should largely be carried out outside the school. As speed in competitions generally lies between 350 and 400 m (380 and 435 yards) per minute, the speed in training does not need to be much greater than this. I recommend riding a stint of 2000 m (2200 yards) at 350 m (380 yards) per minute without a break.

The rider must acquire a sense of speed, and try to maintain the correct speed in training. If the horse has learnt to go freely at the 'endurance canter', one can increase the load by seeking out sloping or undulating ground, and by introducing some cross-country fences into the programme.

Rest periods must be permitted, in order to guard against fatigue and loss of keenness in the horse.

Frequent rides in the countryside not only improve the horse's condition, but also calm his nerves. Riding through forest tracks and over broken ground will act as a gymnastic exercise

Cavaletti and small fences for
gymnastic jumping

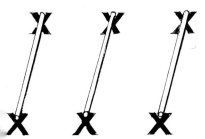

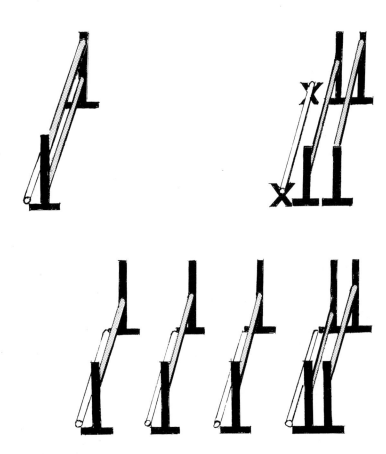

Improving Jumping Power

Power and technical ability
are the two main qualities of
the show-jumping horse. To
increase the horse's capacity
for both will require special
training.
Jumping at a faster speed at
the canter will improve
elasticity and spring, but too
fast a tempo will lead to errors
in accuracy, as the horse is no
longer in a position to control
the angle and motion of the
leg joints. The horse will jump
higher if the speed is reduced,
provided that the approach
does not become so slow that
the horse loses all momentum.
For improvement of jumping
power the best exercise is to
jump out of the trot.
Cavaletti are of great value in
jumping training.
Set up several cavaletti in
front of a fence, with a space

Four riders jumping the same fence—
with very little difference of style and
technique

of 3.50 to 4 m (11½ to 13 feet)
between the last cavaletti and
the fence, which should be at
a height of 90 to 110 cm (3 to
3⅔ feet). The effect can be
increased by building a
combination at a distance of
3.50 to 4 m (11½ to 13 feet).
Jump at the trot at first,
later from the canter; only
increase the height if the horse
jumps relaxed and calmly.
Work up and down hills will
develop the jumping muscles.

Jumping Technique. The
requirements in higher grades
(such as B and A) mean not
only higher fences, but more
difficult courses.
Before the rider can consider
tackling courses at this level
he must be able to regulate
speed and length of stride
either in the approach or
between the fences. Half-halts
(given by driving with the legs
into a restraining hand) cause
the hindquarters to be more
actively engaged under the
horse, enabling the rider to
bring the horse under control
of the aids after it has become
too 'long' in the canter

between fences. Gymnastic jumping will help to reduce resistance in the mouth and poll, so that the half-halts are accepted softly without loss of balance.

Correct approach to the fence is largely determined by the ability of the rider to estimate distance (by 'seeing a stride') and his ability to control the horse, adjusting the length of stride and acceleration in order to arrive at the correct point for take-off.

Gymnastic jumping helps both horse and rider to estimate the correct take-off, from a normal approach distance of three or four strides, depending on the size and nature of the fence. With spread fences built both high and wide, the approach distance will be longer than that for upright fences.

If the rider accelerates too far from the fence, then the horse will not be able to round his back nor fold the legs. The jump parabola will be no longer forwards and upwards, but will become too flat.

Faults

- Half-halts, given jerkily, will cause the horse to evade the aids.
- The rider loses contact with the horse's mouth when accelerating on the approach ('drops the horse').
- The horse thus falls apart and jumps flat.
- Cramping the paces by overshortening the neck prevents the horse from stretching out over the fence.

Different Obstacles and their Effects

A fence is easier to jump when it is built in an inviting manner, that is,

- Well filled-in
- With a clear ground-line
- With the front of the fence lower than the back.

Take-off zone:
Every fence has an optimum zone from which the horse can clear the fence with the minimum of effort. The take-off zone is determined by the height and spread of the fence—the most favourable point is generally one-third the height of the fence from the front of the obstacle.
The higher the fence, the narrower becomes the take-off zone. Arrival at the correct point is achieved by absolute control of the length of stride on the approach.
A combination is defined as two or more fences whose distance does not exceed 11 m (39 ft 4 in under British rules).

Single Fences

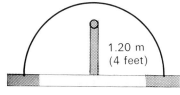

| 1.20 m (4 feet) |
| Take-off zone   Landing zone |

| 1.50 m (5 feet) |
| Take-off zone   Landing zone |

The best distances for doubles and trebles (measured from the middle of one fence to the middle of the next) are 3 to 3.50 m (10 to 11½ feet), 7 to 8 m (23 to 26 feet), 10 to 11 m (33 to 36 feet), 14 to 15 m (46 to 49 feet) (no longer a combination but a 'related distance').
Training for combinations is first introduced into gymnastic

jumping. Here a line of five or six small fences at normal distances is jumped in a regular canter rhythm. Impulsion must be kept up between the fences, but the rider should influence or interfere with the horse as little as possible.
In jumping doubles or trebles the rider must learn to collect his horse after landing

Combinations

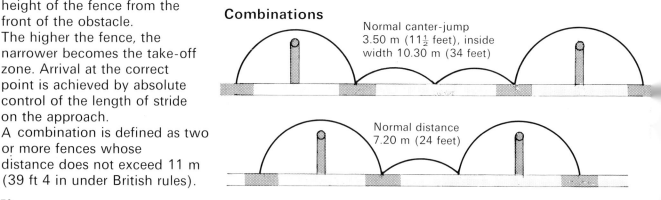

Normal canter-jump 3.50 m (11½ feet), inside width 10.30 m (34 feet)

Normal distance 7.20 m (24 feet)

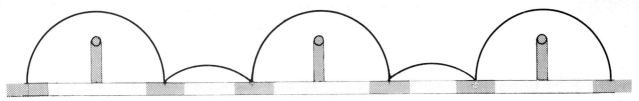

Normal canter-stride 3.50 m (11½ feet)   Normal distance 7.20 m (24 feet)

and lengthen or shorten the normal canter stride—about 20 cm (8 in)—at first, and practise the shortening before the lengthening. Be careful not to ask too much, but to remain within the bounds of possibility—or setbacks may result.

Doubles may consist of the following:—two uprights—upright, spread—spread, upright—two spreads.

Trebles—upright, upright, spread—upright, spread, spread—spread, upright, spread—spread, spread, upright.

The combination of different types of fence determines the difficulty of the obstacle. Distances are graded as normal, short, or long. Normal distance lets the horse retain the tempo after landing; short distance forces the rider to shorten the stride; long distance demands acceleration and a longer stride in order to reach the take-off zone.

Riding-in before a Jumping Competition

Success in the arena depends much upon how the horse and rider prepare outside before the competition. Limbering-up should be based on previous experience and should follow a definite routine. With young horses, especially, or those of difficult temperament, the rider must make allowances for strange surroundings, and the tense atmosphere of competition. If jumping in the afternoon, the horse should be ridden-in during the late morning.

There is no formula which suits all horses; time and method depend on the temperament of the horse—some need a short livening-up, others need a long calming-down. Calculate the work-programme from the timetable and the list of starters—it is better to take plenty of time and allow a 'recovery' period to fill in waiting-time, rather

than be forced to jump after a rushed preparation.

Loosening-up forms the most important part of preparation. Rising trot, repeated changes of hand, canter strike off, and periods of walk will be the normal programme.

This will be followed by exercises to increase *handiness and activity*—that is, transitions at trot and canter, halts, rein-back and turns on the haunches. If the rider can get the horse going freely without lying on the hand, obedience is being achieved.

Practice jumps will follow. Since inviting fences are not often available in the practice area, one should begin with low, broad spreads, and if all goes well, go on to three or four jumps of medium height including at least one upright. Coach, groom, or a friend on the ground can often give good advice as to how well the horse is jumping, and whether he is folding well. Practice jumping should be

Harmony between horse and rider are shown here not only in the arena, but also in practice—the foundation of success

timed to take place as near as possible to the start of the actual round. During the short pause between one and the other, keep the horse on the move at the walk.

Faults. Jumping a practice jump built for someone else— or without sufficient preparation on the ground. If the horse is jumping badly, take care not to tire him or destroy his confidence by repeated failure.

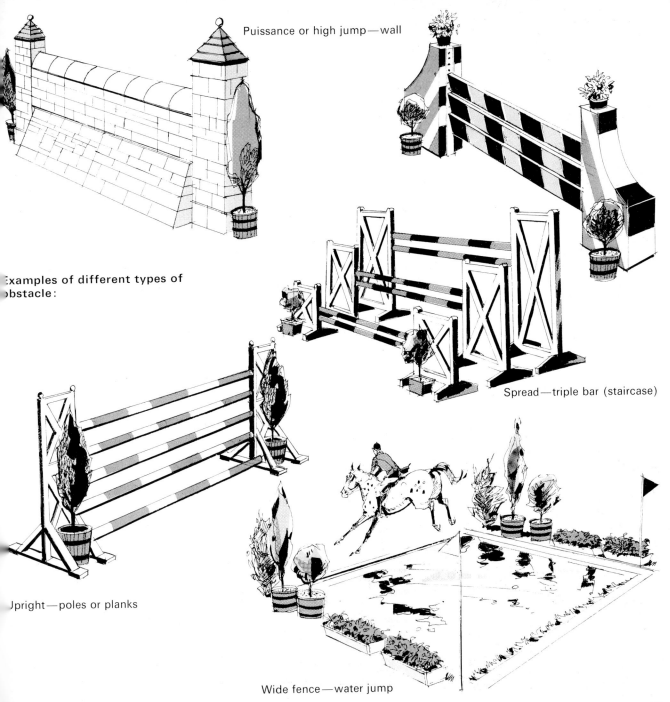

Puissance or high jump—wall

Examples of different types of obstacle:

Spread—triple bar (staircase)

Upright—poles or planks

Wide fence—water jump

The Show-jumping Competition

Walking the course completes the preparation period, which includes not only the limbering-up of the horse and rider, but precise study of the individual fences, and the course as a whole.
As soon as permission is granted, the rider should walk the course, and study the best line from fence to fence—the track will depend on the type of competition (such as, against the clock or not) and the degree of schooling of the horse and rider. The latter will do well to watch some of his rivals on the course, if the starting order allows.
Tactics also dictate the way in which a course is ridden. Young horses should be ridden at an even pace, on the easiest line; later, if horse and rider are in good form, short cuts and bolder riding may be allowed. If a rider has two horses in the same competition he will ride the better one second, thus profiting from the experience of the first round. If it comes to a jump-off, the rider will have the advantage of knowing what he has to beat (the author assumes [as in FEI rules], that the order is not redrawn for the jump-off).

As a rule the rider should trot in and out of the ring. After saluting the judges and receiving the starting signal, he makes a wide circle and approaches the start-line in the tempo desired. The first fence —generally small and inviting —is often approached too slowly, and as a result of passive riding, unnecessary faults often occur at this point. Once on the course, keep calm and concentrate, not only on the separate fences and combinations, but also on the ground conditions underfoot. A clear round up to the last fence may lull the rider into carelessness, but he must ride on well, keeping the horse on the bit, right through the finish. The good horseman will retain a smooth harmonious style from start to finish, in spite of the need for half-halts, checks and corrections. In unexpected situations the rider must keep his head. After a refusal, ride with determination, taking enough room to regain impulsion. After turning away from the fence, a tap from the whip on the flank will help.

The only jumping course (in Germany) which always remains the same:

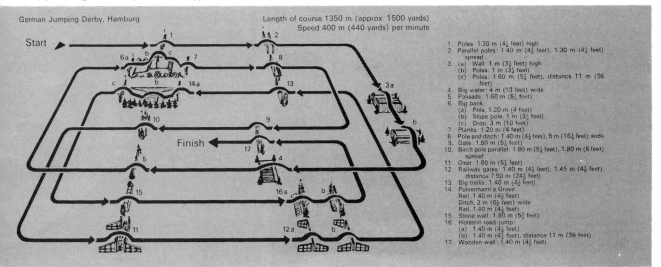

German Jumping Derby, Hamburg

Length of course 1350 m (approx. 1500 yards)
Speed 400 m (440 yards) per minute

Start

Finish

1. Poles: 1.30 m (4¼ feet) high
2. Parallel poles: 1.40 m (4½ feet), 1.30 m (4¼ feet) spread
3. (a) Wall: 1 m (3⅓ feet) high
   (b) Poles: 1 m (3⅓ feet)
   (c) Poles: 1.60 m (5¼ feet), distance 11 m (36 feet)
4. Big water: 4 m (13 feet) wide
5. Palisade: 1.60 m (5¼ feet)
6. Big bank:
   (a) Pole, 1.20 m (4 feet)
   (b) Slope pole, 1 m (3⅓ feet)
   (c) Drop, 3 m (10 feet)
7. Planks: 1.20 m (4 feet)
8. Pole and ditch: 1.40 m (4½ feet), 5 m (16½ feet) wide
9. Gate: 1.60 m (5¼ feet)
10. Birch pole parallel: 1.60 m (5¼ feet), 1.80 m (6 feet) spread
11. Oxer: 1.60 m (5¼ feet)
12. Railway gates: 1.40 m (4½ feet), 1.45 m (4¾ feet), distance 7.50 m (24½ feet)
13. Big trellis: 1.40 m (4½ feet)
14. Pulvermann's Grave:
    Rail, 1.40 m (4½ feet)
    Ditch, 2 m (6½ feet) wide
    Rail, 1.40 m (4½ feet)
15. Stone wall: 1.60 m (5¼ feet)
16. Holstein road-jump:
    (a) 1.40 m (4½ feet)
    (b) 1.40 m (4½ feet), distance 11 m (36 feet)
17. Wooden wall: 1.40 m (4½ feet)

Extracts from the Olympic
Individual Competition (second
round) from the 1972 Games—
Fritz Ligges on Robin

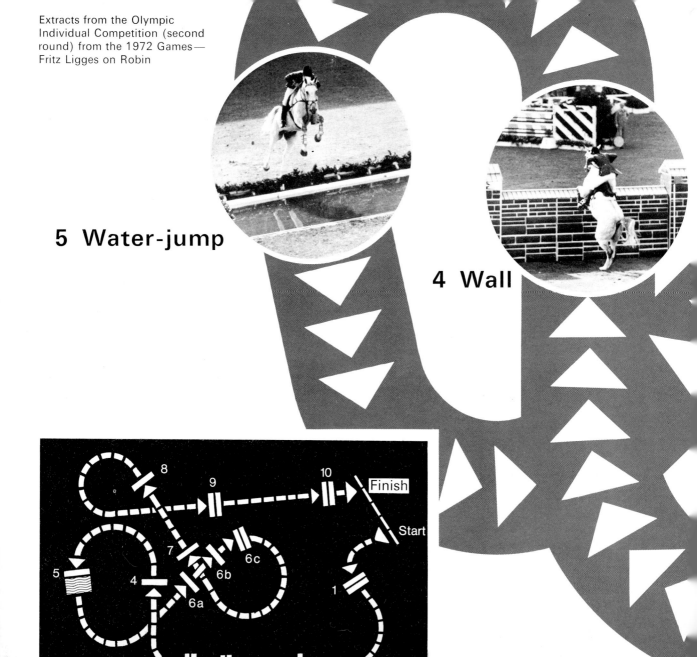

5 Water-jump

4 Wall

6c
6b
6a
Treble
combination

7

a 3b

Double combination

The Three-day Event

The Three-day Event is the summit of the art of riding; it makes the greatest demands on the schooling, fitness, and jumping ability of the horse. The experience needed for a full Three-day Event can only be gained through hunting, hunter trials, horse trials and Three-day Events at different standards.

Horse and Rider for the Three-day Event

The first premise in aiming for the Three-day Event is to choose a horse which is suitable. The half-bred or threequarter-bred has proved to be the best, being of medium size, with clean, sound legs, strong tendons, good nerves, and an uncomplicated stomach. The horse must show good paces, with the ability to gallop on. Only after several years of schooling, when obedience, speed, jumping, and toughness have been tested by results in one-day horse trials, is it wise to attempt the Three-day Event.

Combined training will be chosen by a rider who not only has a suitable horse, but also has experience in both dressage and jumping. The Three-day Event rider should possess a normal rider's figure (not too heavy), and a good supple seat; he (or she) will need nerve, fitness and concentration as well as sympathetic horsemanship. Technical ability and skill may take several years to acquire. Complete mutual trust between horse and rider are essential in a combined competition, especially in the cross-country section.

Combined Training

Combined training consists of dressage, cross-country and show-jumping, and the programme must be conceived as a whole. Dressage will lay the foundation for the other disciplines. Riding out in the countryside supplements work in the manège and jumping arena. Training must consist of a methodical and gradual progression, increasing not only the muscular ability of the horse but also his confidence. One-day Horse Trials should be attempted once the horse is four years old (in Britain the horse must be five years old before competing), and has gained sufficient qualities of endurance, courage, obedience and jumping ability to tackle the cross-country course.

Training for the Dressage Test

A horse is not likely to remain sound unless his paces are relaxed, rhythmical and well-balanced, and he accepts the bridle willingly.

The horse which has been made supple by gymnastic schooling should be able to get his rider out of difficulties. A high degree of collection is not required—compared with that demanded of specialist dressage horses. Nevertheless it is important to develop the activity and engagement of the hindquarters in order to lighten the load on the forehand, saving the strain on the tendons and joints, and preventing the horse from pulling too strongly on the cross-country course.

Dressage should be practised not only in the school or arena, but also in the open while riding out, thus accustoming the horse to different surroundings. Flat fields, wide paths and sandy stretches are ideal for this type of work.

Riding in the arena demands accuracy of control; the individual components of a test should be practised, but the complete test should not be ridden too often.

Cross-country Training

Cross-country makes the hardest demands on the horse for endurance, speed, jumping ability and courage. Training must aim at bringing the horse to the start of the course in the best possible mental and physical state for the test. The rider must assess the ability and immediate fitness of his horse, and ride the course sensibly, and be aware of the factors concerned; training must therefore be particularly careful and thorough.

The winter months should be spent in dressage and occasional jumping over easy fences—including combinations. Outdoor training begins in the spring—generally from March (in Germany). The horse can then be introduced to different types of cross-country fence, the rider taking the opportunity to tackle as many natural obstacles as possible, emphasising a smooth fluent approach, and choosing inviting obstacles of small or medium size.

Judgement of correct speed across country is a vital part of training. An accurately measured distance on good sandy going should be used for slow and half-speed canter work. For galloping, a grass track is preferable.

If an uphill stretch can be included, this will improve the horse's wind, and at the same time lighten the load on the front tendons.

Long-distance Training.

Long-distance training should be included in the cross-country work, the rider learning how to save his horse by alternate periods of slow canter, trot and walk. Hard ground, needless to say, should be avoided if possible. The amount of canter work

should be increased as the horse gains in fitness. Slow cantering up to 4 to 5 km (2½ or 3 miles), at 350 m (400 yards) per minute will help to build the muscles. Short spells of fast work up to 650 m (700 yards) per minute will help to clear the horse's wind. The rider must take care to allow for recovery periods— after every fast canter the horse must be allowed to return to normal breathing. This should not take longer than five to eight minutes. When the horse becomes fit after six to eight weeks of cantering, working up to 650 m

(700 yards) per minute, then endurance training for the steeplechase course is begun.

Endurance Training.

Training for the steeplechase phase should begin with quiet cantering at 400 to 500 m (440 to 550 yards) per minute; once a week will be enough. The less well-bred the horse, the more carefully must the racecourse phase be approached. Once speeds of 600 m (650 yards) per minute are reached, steeplechase conditions should be provided, allowing schooling over small obstacles at first. Too much

galloping will tend to 'hot-up' the horse.

The cross-country course is the climax of any combined event. The horse must be introduced to all types of obstacle, combinations, road-crossings, timber, oxers, ditches, etc., and jumps into water, which often create some problems for horse and rider. Speed between the jumps must be adapted to suit the horse's fitness. This will be shown by his condition—good coat, little sweating, and good appetite. Loss of condition will indicate that demands on the horse are too great.

Steeplechase fences

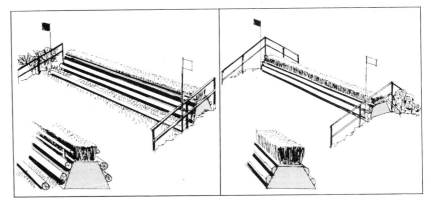

The drawings below show some
obstacles in the Olympic Games in
Munich

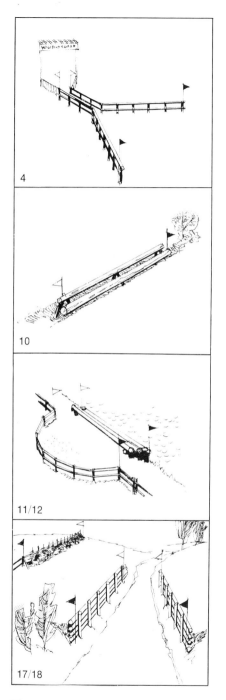

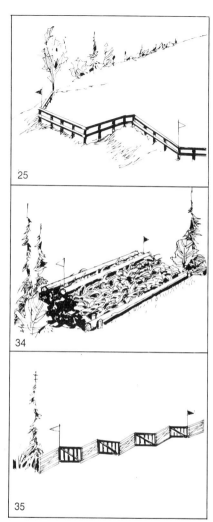

Not all cross-country obstacles can
be practised in training—in every
competition new fences may appear.
Confidence and obedience to the aids
will be the key to tackling strange
fences

Show-jumping Training

The show-jumping test at the end of a Three-day Event is designed to test the condition of the horse. The combined training horse must jump calmly and fluently in the arena, without pulling at the rider. The transition from cross-country course to jumping arena always creates problems—and the rider must therefore practise over coloured fences, as part of his training plan.
Gymnastic jumping and show-jumping competitions should be included in the winter training schedule—competitions up to grade B and C will be sufficient.

After the exhausting demands of the cross-country course, the obedient and supple horse can often gain a few places in the show-jumping section. Here the rider allows himself an unwise backward glance at the fence

1

2

3

4

5

6

One-year Training Plan

[*Translator's note:* The German Eventing Calendar is rather different from ours.]

First Preparation Period:
November to February.
Section 1
The winter months will largely be devoted to dressage, accompanied by schooling over single fences up to 1.10 m (3 ft 6 in), and occasionally over a course of ten to twelve fences.

Section 2
When weather and ground permit, one should start work in the outdoor arena, and across country. Plenty of walking, quiet trotting and cantering, trotting for about 2 km (1¼ miles) at 200 to 300 m (220 to 330 yards) per minute. Take care not to get the horse too hot, especially when he is changing his coat.

Second Preparation Period:
March to April.

Section 1
Start cross-country training. Continue dressage and jumping—riding tests and jumping courses in practice.
Section 2
Cross-country as in March. Canter work to suit the developing fitness of the horse, increasing to 4 to 5 km (2½ or 3 miles) at 350 m (380 yards) per minute. Increase work up-hill, intensive gymnastic jumping together with dressage.

First Competition Period:
May to June.
After three months (March to May) a fit and well-schooled horse should be ready for a One-day Horse Trial, or an easy Three-day Event. If possible, two to three weeks before the Event, take part in two or three competitions of dressage and show-jumping. After the Event, allow a short but active recovery period of four to eight weeks, during which the horse is kept in training.

Second Competition Period: June to July.
Endurance work as in the preparation period, concentrating for the first climax of the year, a full Three-day Event, followed by a short recovery period.

Third Competition Period: August to October.
Continue fitness work, then six weeks preparation for the second climax of the year—a second Three-day Event.

It is important to bring training to an end up to ten days before the Event, then only allow gentle exercise, which keeps the horse in condition but without mental strain. Dressage work in the arena, easy jumping of single fences or small courses, and quiet riding across country will be enough.
At the end of the competition season, the horse should be let down quietly and gradually.

One-week Training Plan

Every combined training rider must make his own training plan, based on the state of schooling and fitness of his horse, and the facilities available—schooling area, cross-country, or gallops. A suggested week's training plan is given here:

Monday
Thirty minutes loosening-up in the school finishing with one-and-a-half to two hours exercise riding out, trotting and gentle canter up to 4 km ($2\frac{1}{2}$ miles), walking and work up-hill; a few single cross-country jumps at a pace of 300 to 450 m (330 to 500 yards) per minute.

Tuesday
One hour loosening-up and dressage in the large arena (20 m × 60 m; 21 × 65 yards). Ride a test or parts of a test, in a snaffle. Jump a few single show-jumps up to 1.20 m high (4 ft).

Wednesday
Thirty minutes loosening-up, followed by work on the gallops, of 1600 to 2000 m (1750 to 2200 yards) fast canter at 500 to 550 m (550 to 600 yards) per minute; recovery by fifteen to twenty minutes walking.

Thursday
Gallop 1200 to 1400 m (1300 to 1525 yards) at about 600 m (650 yards) per minute; two hours gentle walking and trotting on tracks and cross-country. Trotting up to 6km ($3\frac{3}{4}$ miles) at 240 m (260 yards) per minute, uphill if possible.

Friday
Thirty minutes loosening-up, one hour walking and trotting followed by 2000 m (2200 yards) fast canter at 400 to 500 m (440 to 550 yards) per minute with six to eight steeplechase jumps.

Saturday
Thirty minutes loosening-up, one hour quiet hacking; jump a few cross-country jumps at 350 to 400 m (380 to 440 yards) per minute.

Sunday
Rest-day.

Feeding and Care of the Horse

Correct feeding and stable-management are essential to success. The diet must suit the level of work, and be adapted to the requirements and size of each horse. In quiet work 5 to 6 kg of oats (11 to 13 lb) will be enough, together with 4 to 5 kg (9 to 11 lb) of good hay. Turnips and linseed may be added, especially during the period of change of coat. In full training an event horse, which has a good appetite, needs 7 to 8 kg of oats ($15\frac{1}{2}$ to $17\frac{1}{2}$ lb) per day. Horses should be watered before feeding. Loss of appetite may follow, or result in, a drop in performance. The cause may be organic illness, or overtiredness. The coat becomes dull and staring. Work should be reduced and the horse only given quiet exercise for a time, just as if the horse had damage to tendons or joints. Appetite can be stimulated by the addition of molasses, root tops, clover

etc. Take care to feed 'little
and often'.
After work, the back under the
saddle should be washed (in
warm weather), as well as the
legs and feet.
Look carefully for cuts or
bruises, for heat or swelling in
the tendons, and for loose
shoes. Care of the legs is vital,
since everything depends on
the horse remaining sound. As
far as possible always employ
the same blacksmith; while in
light work, the shoes should
be kept at full length in the
heel, so that the foot has full
support.
For final training and for the
competition the shoe can be
slightly shorter, in order to
avoid the danger of pulling off
a shoe.

Studies of different riders over the
same fence

The Competition

The Three-day Event is divided into Dressage, Cross-country and Show-jumping, spread over several days, thus giving the rider plenty of time to prepare himself for each section. Preparatory work for dressage and show-jumping has already been described on pages 48 and 62.

Mark Phillips on Great Ovation, in the dressage test at the Munich Olympics

The Three-day Event Dressage Test

1

A
Enter at collected canter

X
Halt, salute

2

X
Proceed at medium trot (sitting)

C
Track right

M X K
Change rein at extended trot (rising)

3

K A F
Medium trot (sitting)

F X H
Change rein at extended trot (rising)

4

H C M B
Medium trot (rising)

5

B

Turn right (sitting)

X

Halt, 5 seconds immobility
Proceed at collected trot

E

Track left

E K A F

Collected trot

6

F X

Half-pass left

X M

Half-pass right

7

C

Medium walk

H X F

Change rein at extended walk

8

F

Collected trot

K X

Half-pass right

X H

Half-pass left

9

C

Halt, 6 steps rein-back, proceed at medium walk

10

C M

Medium walk

M

Collected canter right

11

F

Half-circle 10 m (33 feet) diameter

B C S

Counter-canter

12

S

Medium trot sitting

V

Collected canter left

13

K

Half-circle 10 m (33 feet) diameter

E C R

Counter-canter

14

R

Medium trot sitting

P

Collected canter

15

K **H** **C**

Extended canter

16

C **M**

Medium walk

M **X** **K**

Change rein at extended walk

17

K

Collected canter left

F **M** **C**

18

C **H** **E**

Extended canter

19

E

Collected canter left

A

Down the centre line

G

Halt salute, leave arena at free walk on a long rein

Collective marks:

Quality of the paces
Impulsion
Suppleness, submission and obedience of the horse
Seat and application of the aids by the rider
Deductions—exceeding the time allowed, half a point for each commenced second

In the show-jumping on the final day the rider must ride absolutely straight at the fences in a quiet but fluent style

Cross-country Technique

In the following picture sequences the author has tried to demonstrate technique on the cross-country course, in a number of different situations. At the Munich Olympics in 1972 the course was very testing to both horse and rider. Study of the photographs may help the less experienced rider to make comparisons with his own style. In any case, the pictures show some of the world's best event riders in action.

Fence No. 3 (above)
Covered deer feeder, 1.15 m ($3\frac{3}{4}$ feet) high, 1.60 m ($5\frac{1}{4}$ feet) spread

After careful study of the cross-country course, the rider must decide whether success is going to depend on the ability to jump very big fences, or whether speed will be the most

important factor. Tactics will depend on the state of the going, and the size and type of the obstacles. Cross-country obstacles often blend into the landscape so that the horse only recognises them at the moment of take-off. Here the rider takes the parallel part of the birch rails

Fence No. 4 (below)
Rustic birch rails, 1.15 m (3¾ feet) high, 1.80–2 m (5¾–6½ feet) wide

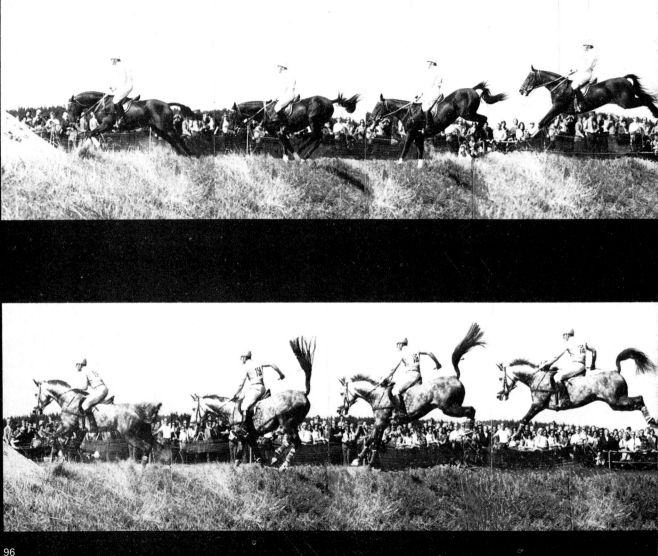

Fence No. 10

Rails and ditch, 4 m (13 feet) wide

The big ditch demands plenty of impulsion, as shown here by both horses. In mid-air the rider gives his horse plenty of rein to allow him to reach out for the far side

Combination fences No. 11 and 12

Rails 1 m (3¼ feet) high, rail into pond 90 cm (3 feet) high, 1 m (3¼ feet) spread, 1.15 m (3¾ feet) drop into water

Up and down slopes, drop fences and jumping into water demand great experience in order to deal with varied conditions of take-off, flight and landing. Speed must be regulated carefully, and for drop

fences, the rider must adapt his seat to the braking effect. In this type of situation unquestioning obedience and reliability are more important than speed.

The grey is too fast into the water, the rider trying to stay in the saddle by sitting back, but on surfacing after the dive, horse and rider have parted company!

Another view of fences Nos. 11 and 12

The rider in the lower picture shows how jumping into water is best achieved without too much impulsion. In the air the back is straightened and braced for the drop, and the rider sits firmly with the lower leg a little forward

Fences Nos. 17, 18 and 19

17a Drop, 1.05 m (3½ feet)
17b Drop into sunken road
18   Rail at top of slope, 1.20 m (4 feet) high
19   Oxer

Approaching the fence horse and rider are obviously alert. A beautiful jump, horse and rider in perfect harmony, with a good landing—a fluent performance over two drops, with the rider sitting very well.

The rider takes the weight off the horse's back for the upward jump. After the right turn the horse is well balanced for the next fence. The rider keeps contact with the horse's mouth, without in any way interfering. The rider's seat throughout the jump is faultless

Fence No. 17 (below)

Rail and drop, 1.05 m ($3\frac{1}{2}$ feet) high

There is no hint of a refusal on the approach, but the horse may possibly be tiring. The rider sits well during the refusal. A second attempt must be made with determination, and a surprise from the whip just before the fence

Fence No. 25 (above)

Rail or slope, 1 m ($3\frac{1}{4}$ feet) high

The rider slows up, in order to give his horse a more collected take-off for the drop. For uphill jumps the rider should increase the speed and impulsion and give his horse a clear indication to take off

Fence No. 34 (below)

Root-clamp, 1.15 m ($3\frac{3}{4}$ feet) high, 1.90 m ($6\frac{1}{4}$ feet) wide

On the level, near the end of the course, the rider can increase the speed. Usually the most difficult fences are found after the first third of the course. Towards the end of the course, there are fewer uprights and more spread fences. Here both riders approach and jump at a steady speed

Physical Training for the Rider

Riding is a complicated sport, demanding fine muscular co-ordination by the rider, in the application of the aids.

A good rider needs a delicate sense of balance, and special muscular development. The rider must be relaxed, and be sensitive to the movements of the horse. Some riders have this 'feel' naturally, others only acquire it through years of training. A comparison of beginners and experts will soon show up the bad position, tenseness and stiffness of the former.

All other sports make use of special gymnastic exercises—why then does not riding? It is better to use exercises than to risk injury. Riding, in a way, demands immobility from the rider, compared with other sports—the expert moves even less than the beginner—and therefore these compensating exercises are suggested.

General Fitness Training

The experienced rider, especially if working several horses each day, is likely to be fairly fit. Yet he must take steps to maintain this condition. Other sports such as swimming will keep the muscles in tone. Correct breathing technique helps relaxation and suppleness of the seat; the rider must combine this suppleness with fitness. Suitable complementary sports are swimming, running, cycling and tennis, among other physical activities. The training programme must be designed to avoid stiffening the wrong muscles.

A test of fitness should be carried out regularly, to check on basic condition (strength, speed, stamina and agility). The help of a colleague is recommended, since while one is doing the test, the other can rest and mark the performance. The test should be conducted calmly, only starting a new section when the pulse rate has returned to normal. Repeat the test every four weeks, noting the pulse rates. The attached table will enable the rider to calculate his or her state of fitness.

General Fitness Test

This list will clearly indicate your condition:

Exercise 1

Jumping over partner, feet together

Test

Muscle power, agility, co-ordination

Exercise 2

Raising and lowering the legs

Test

Strength and endurance of stomach muscles

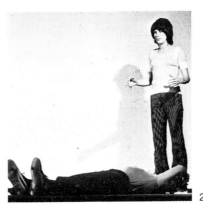

Exercise 3

Press-ups

Test

Strength and endurance of arm, back and stomach muscles

Time: 30 seconds
R = Result (fill in yourself)
M = Male
F = Female

Age		very good	R	good	R	normal	R	Pulse before – after	
Up to 20 years	M	60		55		50			
	F	55		50		45			
20–40 years	M	50		45		40			
	F	45		40		35			
40–60 years	M	40		35		30			
	F	35		30		25			
Over 60 years	M	35		30		25			
	F	30		25		20			

Age		very good	R	good	R	normal	R	Pulse before – after	
Up to 20 years	M	25		23		20			
	F	23		21		18			
20–40 years	M	20		18		15			
	F	18		16		13			
40–60 years	M	18		15		13			
	F	16		13		11			
Over 60 years	M	15		13		10			
	F	13		11		8			

Age		very good	R	good	R	normal	R	Pulse before – after	
Up to 20 years	M	25		23		20			
	F	25		23		20			
20–40 years	M	20		18		15			
	F	20		18		15			
40–60 years	M	18		15		13			
	F	18		15		13			
Over 60 years	M	15		12		10			
	F	15		12		10			

Exercise 4

Raising the torso

Test

Strength of the back
muscles

4

Exercise 5

Jumping up from prone
position

Test

General endurance, speed
and agility

5

Age		very good	R	good	R	normal	R	Pulse before – after	
Up to 20 years	M	25		23		20			
	F	23		21		18			
20–40 years	M	20		18		15			
	F	18		16		13			
40–60 years	M	18		15		13			
	F	16		13		11			
Over 60 years	M	15		13		10			
	F	13		11		8			

Time: 30 seconds
R = Result (fill in yourself)
M = Male
F = Female

Age		very good	R	good	R	normal	R	Pulse before – after	
Up to 20 years	M	12		11		10			
	F	11		10		9			
20–40 years	M	11		10		9			
	F	10		9		8			
40–60 years	M	10		9		8			
	F	9		8		7			
Over 60 years	M	9		8		7			
	F	8		7		6			

Riding Gymnastics

A natural easy seat is made up of an upright but supple spine, relaxed shoulders, elbows held lightly to the sides of the body, and quiet hands; thighs flat, heels down, lower leg making contact with the horse's body. The hips follow the horse's movement, involving the muscles joining pelvis and spine, which must be specially trained.

If we have a horse with a stiff back, we give him suppling exercises. We must do the same with the rider; his muscles must first be relaxed.

Loosening Exercises for Arms, Legs and Torso

Warming-up. *Bending and stretching from the waist, with arms circling forward.*

Exercise. From the upright position, bend briskly forwards, swing both arms to the rear, and bend the knees. Then stand up and throw up the arms, ending with a forward circle.

Arms circling forwards and backwards with knees bending and stretching (both sides and one side).

Exercise. With legs astride, swing both arms in a circle forwards, and then backwards. Each time the arms pass the body, bend the knees deeply.

Leg swinging in a figure of eight.

Exercise. Stand on the ball of the foot, and with the other leg make the biggest possible figure of eight. When done fast, this is an excellent balance exercise.

Leg Exercises

'Wood-chopping'.

Exercise. In the astride position, arms joined above the head, swing the torso rapidly downwards as if chopping wood. Bend the knees at first then straighten them.

Object: to improve the mobility of the hips, and stretch the muscles at the back of the legs.

Widening the legs.

Exercise. By slipping the feet sideways widen the straddle until the inner leg muscles are strongly stretched.

Object: a supple seat, improvement of inner leg muscles.

Trunk bending, cross-legged.

Exercise. Sit with legs crossed, hands behind the head, bend the body forward as far as possible between the legs, until the forehead touches the ground, then straighten up.

Object: stretching and strengthening back muscles, small of the back, and inner thigh muscles.

Strengthening Exercises for Trunk and Legs

Exercise. From the astride position with arms at the sides, turn the trunk to right and left, then change to trunk turning and bending touching the toes alternately—right toe with left hand and so on. Between each bend, straighten up. After several turns, change to side bends left and right, swinging the arm above the head. Finish with trunk turning, swinging the arms in the largest possible horizontal circle.

Shoulder-bridge.

Exercise. Lie on the back, arms to the side, legs slightly apart and knees bent. Raise and lower the pelvis and clap the hands together under the seat, in the rhythm of the rising trot.

Knee exercise.

Sit cross-legged, with both hands on the knees. Press downward strongly for about

twenty seconds, then relax and repeat.

Exercises in Falling Off for Beginners

Roll with legs apart.

Exercise. From the astride position lower the trunk and roll forwards to the sitting position with legs apart. All sorts of forward and backward somersaults, from the halt and the walk, will increase general agility.

General. The list above contains ten exercises. A suggested programme is twenty repetitions of each for men, fifteen for women and younger riders.
Each exercise should be performed carefully and with the necessary pauses. As strength improves, increase the repetitions and shorten the pauses.

Riding Tactics

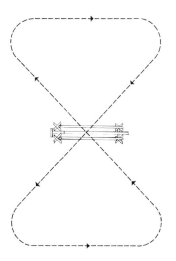

Tactics involve the matching of the demands of competition with the current ability of horse and rider. Success depends on making the most of one's horse, allowing for his limitations and weaknesses. A few notes are given below as a guide:

Dressage

- Correct length of time riding-in
- Making the best of the horse's good points
- Knowledge of the likes and dislikes of particular judges
- In competitions when judging is a matter of opinion rather than fact, a study of the requirements and protocol of judging is essential.

Show-jumping

- Study of the course, course-plan, and careful measurement of distances
- Correct time of riding-in
- Allowance for delays in starting

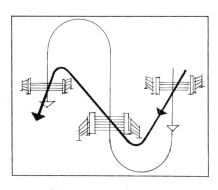

When riding against the clock single or successive fences can be jumped obliquely before or after a turn. This should be practised in training. Note that spreads become wider if jumped obliquely

- Changes dictated by unforeseen events
- Changes of line and track in jumping-off against the clock
- Weighing the odds in a time jump-off—to go carefully or to risk all?

Combined Training

- Careful assessment of the horse's ability before the dressage section. Do not attempt last-minute correction of faulty movements
- Inspection of cross-country course, careful study of each obstacle—approach, take-off and landing areas
- Assessment of speed in relation to going, weather temperature, etc.
- Safety is more important than success
- Adequate warming-up before show-jumping section
- Estimation of reserves of strength left in the horse.

Mental training is of increasing importance—thorough learning of the dressage test and visualising the cross-country and show-jumping courses are all as important as the actual schooling of the horse.